LEAVING HOME WITH HALF A FRIDGE

Arathi Menon spent her childhood in Bangalore where she learnt to love dogs, trees and beer. At the age of thirty-five, she found herself divorced and trying to rebuild a life from scratch. In the process, she rediscovered fun, began to value all the little things that make life such an astonishing gift and got back to writing. Currently, she lives in Bombay and is addicted to happiness and books.

Leaving Home with Half a Fridge is her first book.

She would love to hear from you at halfafridge@gmail.com

You can also follow her on twitter at https://twitter.com/unopenedbottle

LEAVING HOME WITH HALF A FRIDGE

How to Survive a Divorce Happily

Arathi Menon

PAN

First published in the Indian subcontinent 2015 by Pan
an imprint of Pan Macmillan India, a division of
Macmillan Publishers India Limited
Pan Macmillan India, 707, Kailash Building
26, K.G. Marg, New Delhi-110001
www.panmacmillan.co.in

Pan Macmillan, 20 New Wharf Road, London N1 9RR
Basingstoke and Oxford
Associated companies throughout the world
www.panmacmillan.com

ISBN 978-93-82616-39-9

1 3 5 7 9 8 6 4 2

Typeset by Eleven Arts
Printed and bound in India by
Replika Press Pvt. Ltd.

For the guardians of my heart—

My parents, V K Krishnakumari and Narayanankutty—
for love, courage, support. *Always.*

John—
for love and believing I could write.

Contents

III. THE LONG MANICURED HANDS OF LAW

IV. WHAT BREAKS WHEN THINGS SMASH

V. GOING CRAZY ONE DAY AT A TIME

VI. THE MATHEMATICS OF LOVE

PROLOGUE

To Tell a Story You Need to Survive It

Leaving Home with Half a Fridge is an attempt to share a world in which my marriage gets dissolved forever, upsetting every single thing I was brought up to believe in. It is about how I survived this monster called divorce with its many-headed implications, situations, complications and emotions.

It is a chronicle of how I found happiness after the biggest social institution I had committed to had broken down. It is a fairy tale with a happy ending. The only difference is this isn't a story about the prince. It's a story about kissing the wrong frog and its consequences.

I can proudly say that I took care of everything, right from researching about the procedures, fixing the lawyer, attending court to finding my own house and getting my life back on track. Throughout the whole process, my family has supported me wholeheartedly. Their involvement was minimal as they were a state away and I was adamant about handling the situation independently. This didn't stop them from having complete trust in me and my decisions, which gave me the strength to fight and reach my happy place.

I'm sure some of you will wonder about the reason which provoked me to get a divorce. Why did this person end her marriage? Well, this book doesn't answer that. No, it isn't some perverse need to keep your curiosity burning bright. Neither am I holding back a story in the hope of a multi-million prequel deal. It's simply because that story isn't important. What is, is the fact that a divorce happened and there was a survivor who lived to tell her tale.

This is a story of survival, not of destruction.

I hope the misadventures of my divorce will make you laugh, cry, smile and, more importantly, tell you that you are not alone. There are a lot of us out there who are divorced and who are enjoying this new normal. We are chasing happiness, finding meaning, laughing thankfully at the sheer relief of getting a second chance and dancing, passionately, joyfully, unstoppably, to the tune of life.

I

AND THE WORD DIVORCE POPS INTO MY HEAD

The End

I didn't begin my relationship thinking it would end. I wasn't furiously planning for a divorce while sitting in the mandap as the pujari chanted untranslatable, unpronounceable slokas that were supposed to unite us forever. I didn't take the man I married to my parents' house as a temporary guest. Yet, all these things happened. My marriage ended, the slokas didn't work and my parents' think of my Ex as a bad house guest, best forgotten.

No matter what anybody says every divorce is a sad love story. It begins from that one glittering point of excitement, happiness and a lot of hope before the muck piles up so high that it becomes impossible to see even a glimmer of the promised joy. Even today, if I close my eyes, I can hear the declarations of his love. They didn't sound hollow, they were sincere. I know, and he knows. He meant it. Then how did things turn untrue? Was there an expiry date I had failed to notice?

I realized something while going through the divorce. We never ask someone why did you fall in love? When someone loves you and you love them back, you never ask for a reason. You mostly croon back a yes and plan for happiness. Even if there is an answer, it will be a sort of half-truth. Anybody who has experienced the dizzying headiness of a soulmate fantasy knows that love has no reason. It simply is. The reverse is also frighteningly true. You fall out of love, for no reason. It happens, as violently, as suddenly and as unforgivably as falling in love. (Yes, a silent shiver passed down my spine, too.)

In the beginning, I used to talk about the reason I got divorced, almost like a schoolgirl caught by a teacher, 'It wasn't me, Miss'. That has changed now. There is no more blame – there is no point in blame.

'Why' used to be a question that would play around a lot in my head. It would jump up and down, knocking down memory walls, screeching with hysteria, demanding answers. Naturally, it got none. I do not know why some couples stick together and some don't. I used to joke to my Ex that we were more loving to each other while going through a divorce than some married couples we knew.

No matter how malignant, for a lot of us, 'The End' is a reality. The beginning of this end could happen for innumerable reasons.

It could begin when the love you claimed to have, walked out of the door when you weren't looking.

You forgot what had brought you together and focused on what kept you apart.

You realized that if someone walked in and told you the spouse was dead, you would only feel a scary sliver of relief.

Her father, mother, brother, sister, friends took the love you both shared and mangled it so much it began to look like hate.

After he promised to be with you forever, he promptly went and fell in love with an internet bimbo (CallMeHottie) and claimed that she was his soulmate.

He stopped sleeping with you, began sleeping with other people and then brought his shame home and used it to treat you badly.

You were his cover, his camouflage, his greatest lie. The wife to be produced at social functions, to be waved about like a degree certificate and then locked away to gather dust, till it was time to prove to the world again that he was a good, good boy.

He'd hurt you till you began to believe that you deserved only hurt. Then one day someone showed you there was an escape. That it was his fault you were hurt. Not yours.

You couldn't lie to yourself. The love, you loved had died and in the quiet of that carnage the only thing you could hear were two words, 'move out'.

Boredom crept into your veins and froze your passion. You tried everything to thaw it, but the only thing that worked was another person.

You didn't have kids, you had kids, you had too many kids – the happy family wasn't happy.

When the love mist cleared from your eyes, you realized you were chalk and he was cheese. The opposites, fighting physics, began repelling instead of attracting.

There was nothing left between the both of you. Zero. Zilch. Emptiness. Kaput. If you didn't get out of it, this black void would suck you whole and make you as empty as the relationship.

You tried and tried and tried and tried and tried and tried. Now you were tired.

There was no reason. It was over and there was nothing anybody could do about it. You could either choose to live in this hell of meaninglessness or take every ounce of courage you had and snap the threads that held you away from your happiness.

It doesn't matter, the 'why' never does. The sad fact is a lot of marriages are breaking up. We see it everywhere and to view it through the lenses of yesterday's tradition is incorrect. My divorce, while tragic was never melodramatic. It was real and sad and at times, even funny. This is that account, anchored in today's reality and spoken in a language that is ours.

Hide and Search

Unlike a lot of boys, and some girls, I have never looked for porn online or, come to think of it, anywhere else. I have never had to learn how to search for something on the net surreptitiously. I've never been ashamed of the information I needed. This changed when I started thinking about getting a divorce.

Being a law-abiding citizen, I didn't know a lawyer and for some reason I didn't have a single lawyer friend. Maybe I had cracked too many jokes about them. I was in a bit of a spot. I was thinking of getting a divorce and I hadn't the foggiest idea of how to go about it.

When you marry someone, it is serious. It is not like living-in or dating. I don't mean the romance or the relationship: I mean the breaking up. If you want out of the marriage, you can't throw the iPhone he gifted you at his coconut head, pack your suitcase, walk out and go on a blind date. A court stands in the way. A large, legal one, decked up in black robes. When you're getting married, you hardly realize it (unless it's a Special Acts Marriage). They make you sign a register and you blindly do so. In fact, at that moment you'd sign anything as long as you were allowed to rush home and unpin that ton of flowers from your head. A few months later, the marriage certificate comes and it's shelved away along with your tax returns.

Things with the Ex were going downhill and the word 'divorce' kept popping up in my head. I had to find out what it entailed. It wasn't like my mum had dandled me on her knee and explained the divorce laws in India when I was sixteen, along with the 'All boys are bad' lecture. I couldn't talk to a single person I knew for they would want to know the entire backstory and I couldn't fool anyone with 'It's for a friend'. Well, I did what most of us do when we have to research about something we are ashamed of. I went to the God of internet, Google.

A lot of information came up and I must say I was impressed. The problem was I had a memory like that fish in the movie, *Finding Nemo*, and I knew I'd forget critical points. I couldn't favourite the page, in case the Ex saw it. So I copy-pasted the ones I wanted to remember and emailed them to myself and wrote in the subject line: 'Sylvia Plath's Poetry'. I knew the Ex would run a mile from an email like this. You see, I was a bit paranoid. It wasn't like he had my email password but in case my mailbox was open and he glanced at the emails – I wanted my ammo on divorce to be well-hidden. Poor guy, in retrospect, I'm sure he would have never looked at my inbox. At that time, he was too mindf***ed to do anything. After the research, I'd go to the history and delete my finds. It gave me such a sense of triumph to click on 'Clear History' and watch three hours of browsing vanish without a trace. Ta-daa! I felt like a clever spy.

Once, while I was deleting my browser history, the Ex saw me and frowned. I thought I was caught and he was going to ask what I was hiding. I wondered if it was too soon to mention the 'D' word and thought about how I was totally unprepared to do so.

He leaned over my computer and said if I didn't want anybody to see my searches I should browse in private. It was amazing. The computer guys had actually put in an option, which you could click, and it would allow you to look for things in a way nobody would ever know. Private browsing never showed up in your history. Of course, it doesn't say very nice things about the planet we live in, but how wonderful.

From then on, I happily and gleefully searched. It was so liberating, I read blogs, case studies, lawyer forums; I globetrotted across every divorce site the net spewed up – all on a private browser!

Soon I had all the ammunition I needed to make an educated decision. I figured a mutual consent divorce would be the best for us. The Ex and I had to be living apart for a year before we could file for it and after that, six more months were given for the couple to change their minds. During that time, there would be counselling, etc. (This law has changed now.) It's strange, isn't it? You have to go through a process that lasts a year and half to get divorced, while to get married, you need to wait only a month.

Now that I knew what was legally in store for me, it didn't seem that bad. It seemed like a long process, longer than our courtship but they were not going to put anyone in prison or anything. You may laugh at this but you must remember, I never had any dealings with the law before. I had no idea about the divorce process. The only person in my family who had got a divorce was a cousin. I used to hero worship him when I was tiny and impressionable (maybe therein lies the problem) and he lived 'abroad'. In my family, that in itself is an explanation for a lot of things.

Theoretically, however, I was clear. A mutual consent divorce was the most painless. The emotional trauma would be there, but that was my cross to bear. The next question was whether I wanted to get one, or more specifically, whether 'we' wanted to get one. I guess you know the answer to this.

Drop It on the Living Room Carpet

We weren't the kind of couple to brandish the 'D' word every time we had a fight or one of us broke the great grandmother's teacup or forgot to pay the electricity bill in order to better socialize with the Bombay mosquitoes. In fact, the first time it was said was when it was meant to be said. A lot of things could be pronounced as lacking in our marriage, but one of the things it had was a brutal honesty. An unflinching look at facts. It had nothing to do with principles. I think it was because both of us didn't know how to lie convincingly.

What the Ex had done was that he had brought home this big, large problem. He had kept it in our living room and it had started getting bigger and bigger, pushing our marriage out. We both knew it was killing our 'till death do us apart' vow, but he didn't know how to throw it out. I definitely didn't want to stay in a place where everything I believed in was being choked into nothingness. In fact, on some days, I couldn't even see the Ex, for the problem had grown so huge.

Finally, it came to a point where our marriage had almost disappeared. That's when I dropped the 'D' word on the carpet. It fell with a deafening clatter on the problem and immediately, much to my satisfaction, the problem already began to look smaller.

The Ex seemed a bit shocked, like he had never heard the word before. What did he expect? Maybe he thought the problem was like the stench of fish in the locality we had moved into. Over time, we had stopped noticing the smell and used to wonder why new visitors wrinkled their noses in our house. Hah! This smell hadn't just invaded my nose, it had seeped into my brain, permanently clogging some bits, ensuring that I would never forget it.

He sat down and I carefully took him through the process. After the explanations, much to my surprise, he cheered up immensely. He was relieved that the divorce wouldn't happen tomorrow. There was a whole year and half to go through and being the optimist he was, he thought anything could happen by then. He suggested living apart like the courts asked and, pointing at the problem, muttered hopefully that maybe this separation would cause it to disappear. A lot of couples fake this step and pretend they have already lived apart in order to get the divorce more quickly. We, like I said before, were a by-the-rule-book couple (though, clearly, we had missed the manual on marriage).

The problem with having uttered the 'D' word is that it is a monster. It clings to you and grows in power. Every single day, every single minute after you have discussed it, it hangs in your mind.

I used to look at other couples and try to guess whether they were thinking of a divorce. I'd observe the divorced ladies in office and see if there was anything different about them. I'd look at wedding cards and wonder what the fate of these two people, who were going to tie the knot with such optimism, would be.

As my mind swam in the abyss of negativity, a best friend of mine decided to get married. The Ex and I agreed not to tell her and spoil her happy time. It was a terrible charade of togetherness. On the first day of the wedding functions, we walked in dolled up and pretty as a happy picture. It was only when someone paid me a compliment that the Ex realized that I had had a drastic haircut, from ponytail to pixie. His confused acknowledgement, the half-hearted compliment, friends ragging him about being a 'typical' husband, all of it rang false, giving some of our more perceptive friends the first clue that our beautiful world had started developing cracks. Luckily, my best friend was too busy being radiantly happy to notice.

We did everything couples do during that function. It was almost like we were in a play. Her wedding venue was the stage where we'd be with each other, laugh, sit and eat together and when we walked out of the venue the play would end. The dark silence between us sat quietly in the taxi and once we reached our house, we walked into two different bedrooms, strangers till the next day when, once again, we would hand out our free, empty smiles to another audience. Like switches.

Happy, loving couple.

Switch.

Dead, cold individuals.

For a long time after the 'D' word was mentioned, I didn't do anything, I didn't take the next step. We'd wake up in the morning, avoid the problem and go to work. We'd eat dinners silently. Two people sitting across a table and the only sound you could hear was the listless chewing of tasteless food as neither person had felt like dealing with the cook. They had other important things to do, like sulk.

During this time, the date of our wedding anniversary popped up. Perhaps we were trained robots, but we actually tried to do an anniversary dinner in a restaurant. A feeble attempt at normalcy. We sat in this very posh place, barely tasting the chef's specialities, waiting for the evening to get over. I remember we toasted to being 'dysfunctional' and roared with laughter – the relief of being able to laugh at something, even ourselves. In between, there were phone calls from loved ones, cheerfully wishing us 'Happy Wedding Anniversary'.

How hollow that evening was, reeking of everything that was fake. Our lives began to feel like a mockery for when people see a couple, nobody assumes things are terribly bad between them. In fact, the world is so made that a couple is considered a single happy unit. They are referred to as one and plans usually include both people. I used to get annoyed with my friends who would chirrup, 'Say hi to the Ex'. Like a disgruntled old woman, I would mutter under my breath after hanging up about why they wanted to say things to the Ex. After all, they were my friends.

I lived in this world of suspended reality long enough to fear that if I didn't make a move, I would stay here forever. We can get used to anything. Even bone-biting unhappiness can become a normal way to live. In fact, time has a way of tranquilizing you so that shaking off the stupor of sadness to move towards happiness becomes a gigantic effort.

However, the fact that the 'D' word had been said helped. By growing louder and louder, it began pushing me out. The house we shared got unbearable. It hurt so bad to be with someone with whom every single connection, bond and love was broken. The edges weren't just frayed – they were neatly sliced off, leaving cold disconnections and a yawning space between two people who had once promised to be together, forever.

I knew it was time for me to leave and the word 'divorce' was coming with me.

Shoulders to Bawl on

I had been coming here since I was 16. Twenty years later nothing had changed, including the waiters. Their wrinkled, weathered faces were ageless. After I had decided about the divorce, I had a sudden need to tell my best friends about it. I craved for a sort of ratification that I was doing the right thing. I had to reach out to people who would implicitly support me like they had supported every madcap venture of mine, with enthusiasm and love. I flew down to meet my childhood friends, who still lived in the city we had grown up in. Both of them were married with children. I was the wild one of the group but that didn't make them love me any less.

I had rung them up and said that I wanted to meet to tell them something important. They came with a big smile on their lips and bucketfuls of advice. After our hug, both of them shrieked together, 'Do it'! I was dumbstruck, not just by their 'clairvoyance' but their obvious approval. Somehow, I didn't think a divorce would rate highly on their things-to-do list.

Further investigation revealed that they thought I was pregnant and I was wondering whether to keep the baby. Hmm. I could metaphorically term the damn marriage a wee baby.

They listened quietly and with a lot of pain. Ever gone through that? It's your problem, you're the one who is supposed to be suffering but you end up comforting the listener, saying, 'Don't worry, it will be fine. I will get better. There, there, don't cry.'

At some point, I felt like yelling and telling them I was the one with the heartbreak, they were supposed to be my strong, silent support. They got there eventually, after a lot of comforting.

In the beginning, they tried calling me every day, desperately not knowing how to deal with it. Finally, I told them to back off when they called for the fifth day in succession and having nothing better to talk about asked me what I was making for dinner. I assured them I would contact them if I needed anything or if I was in trouble. This seemed to calm them a bit and the calls slowed down to a trickle.

Telling them so made me realize I didn't need anybody's support. This thing that I was going to enter into was a place where I had to be the strongest. I knew that instinctively. I had to shape and lead and control my own sorrow for nobody else would be able to handle it.

The next problem was to tell our mutual friends. We hadn't told anybody yet, though some of them may have guessed. One of the reasons nobody was informed was that there was a hope that things may turn right. If it did, it would be horrible to have aired our dirty laundry in public. We didn't want to be that couple who had-a-problem-but-were-now-back-together; we just wanted to be that couple.

This gentle deception was not appreciated. From a mortified 'I can't believe it' to 'We could have helped if you'd told us earlier' to delayed counselling, which in a sense was the worst for we had already made up our minds and whatever was being said sounded trite and hollow. We had heard the words in our heads a thousand times, 'Compromise, adjust, forgive, time-will-heal, marriage-is-not-a-child's-game, work-it-out', the banal list can go on and on. They were not telling us anything new. We had gone through the logic of these sentences, played them out and briefly even believed in them. It hadn't made a difference, not even an iota.

A few friends said they had expected as much. When I enquired why, they said I would never talk about the Ex. When questions were asked about him, I'd give cursory answers. It's strange how you don't recognize your behaviour till someone points it out to you. I knew the reason why I never spoke about the Ex to these people. They were friends I didn't want to lie to, and by saying nothing I thought the truth wasn't being harmed.

There was a couple we knew who had started dating at the same time as us and who had married a month before us. When we told them, I saw the fear on their faces. They held hands instinctively, relieved that they were together. I'm sure that night they would have gone home and hugged each other tight, as if to ward off the evil that may break them. That night I slept alone, quite cheerfully.

Some friends quietly listened, hugged me, said nothing, or if they did they offered practical advice. 'I know a good house broker', 'Do you have enough money? I can tide you over', 'Go for long walks. Get your insurance done. Go out on weekends. Don't stay at home and brood. Call me, I'll pick you up', 'I made some biryani for you'. They were the best kind, the ones who came with survival tips when you were saying goodbye to the life you had known.

A college friend of mine had fallen in love and was planning to go to Goa with him. As soon as she heard of this update in my life, she caught a flight, made the distance disappear, and came home bringing her man along. I have no idea what he thought about his romantic interlude turning into a show-of-support session, but this impulsive generosity is something I will forever carry with me and be grateful for.

Looking back, I realize how lucky I was to have friends and such a corpus of them. In a divorce, you always walk alone, but it's great to know that as you walk, there are people who will walk a while with you.

One Small Step for Me, One Giant Step for Mommy

Telling the Ex we needed to get a divorce was perhaps easier than telling my parents. I am the pride and joy of my folks. They think I am the best thing that has happened to them. Such adulation is easy when there are no siblings to beat for the spotlight. My parents, actually make that my mother, wanted me to get married ever since I could remember. This wasn't one of those conventional 'the-girl-must-get-married' kind of sexist worries. In fact, it was a bit more morbid.

She felt that since I was an only child, after the death of my father and her, there would be nobody to take care of me. For some inexplicable reason, she thought that a mere husband would fix that unfillable vacuum. Even today, it is relatively easy for me to speak about the passing away of my parents into the world of no return having heard my mother chant it so many times. I can quite effortlessly say, 'When my parents are no more...'

When I got married, the mother of the bride was glowing with more happiness than the bride. Imagine telling this woman that her reserve-parent wanted to retire. He couldn't take on the job she had so trustingly entrusted him with. After this news, I knew that the emotion of 'fear about the future', which dominates most middle-class households, would start mushrooming before long; looming large and hanging like an unmovable cloud. My fear was that this cloud would transfer to me and I would carry it back, which would retard my chances of survival.

I chose the week before New Year's to go home and spill the crushed, twisted and rotting beans. It seemed symbolic, for then the next year would be one of truth. No more lying about how fine my husband and I were.

The minute I entered home, post the usual hug, I thulped a meal extraordinaire. Crabs, raw mango curry, prawn chutney, ghee rice, the essential papad-pickle-curd and an unexpected treat – my mum had tried her hand at making caramel custard for I was insanely fond of it. The custard had turned out superbly. I polished off two bowls. This was normal homecoming fare but I did this simply because if I had spoken before lunch, my mother wouldn't have eaten at all.

The postprandial conversation was painful. As I sat her down and told her about the separation, I watched her face change, but not too much. Surprise, surprise! She confessed she had always suspected something was amiss (can't keep anything from Mother) but she had waited for me to speak about it first. Strategically, my eldest cousin called. This was pre-planned. I felt my cousin's words would add weight and give my mother comfort as the cousin was older, 'had-seen-the-world', mother of two and was respected by the family for her commonsensical and practical approach to things. I don't know what she told her but my mother did seem a lot stronger and more composed about the news afterwards. Once I had reassured Amma that my job was safe and I could take care of myself, her practical worries stopped. The emotional ones began. The next few days were strange.

She spoke to her eldest sister and together they plotted and planned my happiness. My mother decided that she would come back with me to Bombay and speak to the Ex. I agreed.

In retrospect, that was a smart move. Once she met the Ex and spoke to him, she realized what a lot of sh*t her beloved daughter had been putting up with. Nothing bonds people together as much as a common enemy. My mother stopped feeling sad about me and started feeling furious with the Ex. But people of that generation are essentially brought up to be gentle and civil, so her extreme anger, such as it was, was a sigh.

The next problem was how to tell our people, the extended family. I offered to do it for her. I told her I'd call them after work. But she couldn't wait; if she held on to such an enormous secret any longer, her heart would burst. By the time, my workday was over, her immediate family knew.

She said her apprehension of telling her three brothers and sister evaporated after she had told the first two. It must have been a terrible thing for Amma, who was brought up to be conservative, to tell her peers that her daughter was getting a divorce. I thought of this unfamiliar English word, rolling around her tongue with difficulty, getting stuck in her throat, its taste foreign and bitter.

I was a bit worried my uncles and aunt would call and demand an explanation. Carefully and consciously, I coached my mind to be calm, to not get angry, and to remember that these people loved me. To their credit, none of them did call.

I met them much later, after the divorce had come through, at a family function. Each one of them came up to me and shook my hand. It was such a beautiful symbol of solidarity and support. Nothing was said, yet everything was expressed. I was family. I was a child of the family and they were with me, every step of the way.

My father doesn't play a major role in this narrative for when I told him, he said, 'If you want to study further, I will support you.' And 'Be bold'. From him I got a sense that it wasn't a big deal. It didn't matter, whether I was married or not – life had much more to give. He was the only one who treated this emotional catastrophe as a minor mite in my eye.

By doing so, I think he gave me the greatest courage a father could give his daughter. He taught me that there are more important things in the world than a marriage. What happened was as inconsequential as the man who caused it. Looking back, I remember he never asked about the Ex, never referred to him or the marriage, unlike my mother, who continued calling the Ex 'a donkey' in Malayalam for over a year.

My father had taught me many things – to speak the truth, to be well-mannered, to love books, to follow my inner principles, to be kind and compassionate, to never break the law, and to take a vitamin tablet every day. Little did he know, though, that his most wonderful gift was his attitude and I learnt by example. His treating of the Ex as a minor inconvenience, as a nobody, taught me the most valuable lesson I needed to survive the divorce – the importance of myself and the unimportance of the Ex. And that strategy, more than anything else in the world, is what made me survive beautifully.

Moving towards Another Reality

Decisions had been made. Words had been thrown in the air and they had been accepted. As I contemplated the next steps, I thought about what it would mean to go through a divorce. I was so naive when I had made this list, but anyway, here it is.

I would have to learn to stop saying, 'My husband'. Do you know how many times this phrase is used when one is married? I counted seventeen one day.

I'd have to be cool about dirty jokes and not think they had a sexual implication. I couldn't turn into that hysterical touch-me-not.

I took off my wedding band and knew I'd miss playing with it. I used to like to turn it around on my finger, drum it on the table. It was almost as bad as giving up smoking; I didn't know what to do with my hands. For a long time, the untanned mark of the ring would be a prominent symbol of my new status. One day, without me noticing, it faded into my skin, unlike the memories.

Now, I am a strong, independent woman, who is a bit of a chicken, especially when night falls and I'm alone at home. I realized with a growing horror that moving out would mean that there would be nobody to investigate an imagined or, god forbid, real 'noise'. It would all have to be done by me. I thought about buying a can of pepper spray.

I used to have a habit of losing things – my phone, my purse and on the rare occasion, my mind. As a precautionary measure, the Ex had made me sit down one day and memorize his phone number. He was constantly scared that I'd anger the underworld and wouldn't know how to call for help as I would have lost my phone along with its contents. Thus, as luck would have it, the only number I had for emergencies was that of a man I was leaving. Quickly, I memorized my mother's number. I had no clue how that would help either. She was a state away and had no known experience in the 'rescue people from goons' department.

The thing about being with someone is that you never have to think about making plans. There is always someone to go with for that movie, to that new restaurant, or that weird play where everybody moans. I knew once I started living alone, if I wanted company I'd have to ask other people. From I've-booked-tickets-come-to-Regal-at-7 to umm-are-you-free-for-a-movie-today? This transition seemed so frighteningly lonely.

I wondered how I'd buy fruit. This sounds silly, but when I was growing up my dad used to buy the fruit, choosing in-season, ripe-in-the-right-way, the freshest, the plumpest, the juiciest and the tastiest ones for me. After I started living on my own, I stopped having fruits altogether. Then I met the Ex and when I told him this, he took on the fruit-buyer's mantle. Suddenly, I was again faced with a no-fruit-buyer reality. This time, however, I decided I wouldn't be dependent and I'd pick, buy and eat my own fruits. I hold board meetings; surely I could buy things that fall off trees.

I'd have to learn to deal with randy neighbours and other characters who behaved seedy. I do not know why, it's almost like a male code. If you are with a guy, even if he is short, thin, a single-breath-could-blow-him-away type, another man won't bother you. (Not that the Ex was any of these, but this male code puzzled me.)

By now you might have figured, I'm a bit of a klutz when it comes to technology. If you haven't, consider this the confession. Moving away meant I'd have to connect appliances, figure out what was wrong with light bulbs, and decipher why the fridge was making burping noises. I began panicking when a friend gently reminded me about the set of people called 'electricians'. Of course.

I'd have to be okay about sleeping alone and I don't mean this in a sex-starved maniac way. When the Ex used to go out of town occasionally, without me, I'd miss the rhythm of his breathing, that quiet assurance that someone who loves you is next to you, alive and, yes, maybe snoring. The silence of a room where the only breath you can hear is yours, at least for me, is painfully numbing and during these times my heart would crash to my toes. Now, my heart would have to start learning push-ups and get back to where it belonged.

My bills would double, which till now had been halved. I was truly grateful to my parents who had brought me up as an individual, working woman who had the education and the confidence that enabled her to walk out of the door and start a new life without being dependent on anyone. Except electricians, of course. And yes, the finance would pinch, bite and chomp away at my retirement plan but money, unlike time, could be made again.

The only good part about this entire list was food. The Ex was a vegetarian and I loved to eat anything that moved. It would be so glorious to order pork, beef, prawns, duck and their spare parts. Bring on the livers, kidneys, brains, fish eggs and everything else I had missed out on! I had dreams of wiping out dynasties of crabs, gorging on pink strips of bacon for breakfast, ordering mutton biryani and Syrian beef fry every single day. Yum!

That's it. That's what I thought about when I started thinking of moving out and being alone. It seems ludicrously stupid now. I didn't realize I had only scratched the surface of the million things I'd need and feel. The odyssey I was going to go on had so many other adventures in store for me that were going to be gut-wrenching, soul-twisting, heart-bursting, life-changing and earth-shattering. And here I was, worried about who would buy me fruit!

II

STAYING APART TO STAY TOGETHER

Finding the Perfect House to Replace the Imperfect Man

For the last five years, I had never looked for a house alone. I was almost tempted to ask the Ex to come along as I began my house-hunt – the first step of separation – but even I knew that was a stupid thing to do. So I set off on my own, every day after work.

The first broker said he'd meet me outside my current house. I told him I was staying with a cousin. I couldn't tell him 'this is actually my house but my husband and I have decided to separate, yes-it-is-so-sad, but I need to look for a new place,' etc., could I? The tangle of lies had begun.

He looked at me and was impressed by my innocent face and good-job in good-company credentials. Immediately, he took me to a breathtaking flat on Malabar Hill. It faced the sea and was gorgeously furnished. My kingdom would be this large, plush one-bedroom. The catch? I had to be a 'flatmate' to a nonagenarian.

He was a charming man whose children were abroad. Articulate, friendly and cultured, he was someone I'd love to have spent an evening talking to, but sharing a flat with him was a bit much. Especially when he added that he hated having dinner alone so he expected his 'house guests' to have 'suppah' with him. I mumbled my polite goodbyes, picked up my skirts and ran.

I yelled at the agent. I told him I was not sharing my flat with a man, no matter how old and harmless. The agent promptly took me to one with an eighty-year-old woman. Again gorgeous sea view, plush, unthinkable Mumbai heaven, but photographs of Goddess Kali plastered the walls of the flat. The woman came out in a pink nightie, with glazed eyes. Saying it was spooky is an understatement. On our way down, we met a maid, who told us that 'Madam' was very nice; only sometimes she goes 'off'. I decided not to stay with her and find out what that meant, no matter how curious I was.

I fired the agent and got a new one. Here, I was a bit more explicit. I said that I wanted to live alone and my budget was X. He whizzed off on his scooter and my taxi followed in a keen chase. We stopped at a weather-beaten building, but that was okay. A painted building in Bombay is an endangered species, rarely sighted. We climbed four floors as the building was built before they had invented elevators. However, I was thinking, this would be the daily exercise I'd need. It was an attractive, airy place and I was happy. Then I met the owner. 'No non-veg. No boys. No loud music. No coming home after 8 p.m. No plants or pets. No drinking. No putting the dustbin out. No using toilet flush after ten.' (Something to do with an overhead tank, a dripping ceiling and a political party member.) In my head, I added, 'No taking up this house. No living here.'

I further sharpened my brief. I told the agent I worked in the media, my colleagues who were boys would come home and, as the media had unspecified hours, I couldn't have a curfew. I wanted a house with: 'No rules'. Phew.

He scratched his dandruff-ridden hair and as the flakes fell, he said, 'Let me see. You free today for disco?' I fled.

In office, as I was lamenting my house-hunting woes, a colleague gave me the number of another agent. To this one, I added I would need to see a tree from my window. He didn't laugh, god bless him, and found me the most beautiful one-bedroom with a small, luxurious balcony that looked out on a spot of sky. It was on the sixth floor and below me there were trees. It had none of those ugly grills Bombay flats usually have and was filled with sunlight and air. I wasn't worried about safety. I reasoned that any thief who could climb six floors couldn't be kept away by a few thin iron bars.

Then he told me the price. My heart dropped to my knees and I ranted at the agent telling him that it was cruel of him to show me dream flats beyond my budget. He was unperturbed, as though he had been dealing with hysterical women all his life, and asked me to meet the owner. He was confident something would work out.

The owner was a twenty-four-year-old who called me 'Ma'am'. I was almost tempted to give him an owner-tenant power equation lecture but why spoil a good thing, eh? Hearing my earnest 'I'll-take-care-of-the-flat' promise and the fact that I worked for a 'prestigious' company, he gave me the place at the rate I wanted. I almost kissed the agent and the landlord on their cheeks. I'm sure it was my Mallu reserve that prevented this heartfelt show of affection.

The catch? Of course, there was a catch. Something this good couldn't come without strings. It was right next door to the Ex. I could see 'our' old house from my balcony. Every single friend I spoke to advised me to take another place. I ignored their warnings. I had fallen in love with the flat. I didn't care where the flat was located. It was perfect and given the hectic Bombay lifestyles we had, it would be rare that I'd bump into the Ex. Even if I did, so what? It would teach me civility, tolerance and forbearance. I would curb my impulse to murder him.

There was another reason. I was stubborn. I wouldn't let the Ex make my life more difficult than it already was. The flat was exactly what I wanted and just because it had the misfortune of being situated adjacent to the Ex's place, I wasn't going to give it up. He had stolen enough of my happiness and he wasn't going to get this too.

There was a third reason, which I can admit only in retrospect. The Ex and I cared for each other, and as wimpy and needy as it may sound, I felt safer that I was close to him. In case there was an emergency, I'd yell and he'd be there to fulfil the 'protect' part of his failing marriage vows a building away.

Later that evening, I showed the Ex the flat. He loved it and said very magnanimously it was even better than the one we had. Worm!

Leaving Home with Half a Fridge

I signed the agreement for my new home in a flourish of excitement, hoping for the best. Looking at the amount I would be paying every month, I was almost tempted to marry my young owner but I restrained myself. I knew what trouble a marriage could be. For a month after that, I did – nothing. A deep lethargy was eating me and not letting me move. I couldn't force myself to stir out of the house I had to leave. The thought of abandoning this house we'd built together over five years made me numb. I tackled the problem very successfully – I avoided it.

During one of those limbo days, the Ex and I had a trivial fight, which naturally, given the gook we were going through, blew out of proportion. I stormed into the bedroom I was sleeping in and said that I'd shift that very night. Fuelled by anger and pride, I called the movers and packers and soon found myself next door with cartons of books – that was the only thing I had taken from the house. That night I slept on a bed the owner had kindly left behind. It was very romantic and back-breaking. I suppose the owner wasn't an 'only-the-best-mattress-will-do' kind of guy. Then friends came to know and the gifts arrived. A futon, an air conditioner, a mixer-grinder, a fridge and a yummilicious homemade cake. They sat me down and tried to convince me that I should go back to 'our' house and take linen, vessels and the washing machine. They tried to tell me that it was only 'fair' that I took half the things as I would have definitely contributed to buying some of them.

I refused. I was always bad at mathematics and this division didn't seem logical. Also, a single house usually had one fridge, one washing machine and one microwave. I couldn't possibly saw them into halves, could I? I was very uncomfortable with how to go about it. There seemed to be no clear route. What was the fairness quotient while dividing? He keeps the washing machine so I get to keep the fridge? Does this mean a microwave equals a mixer? It didn't make any sense and it seemed, well, petty. I had given this man all of me. When he didn't value that, how would he know the value of half a fridge?

In typical fashion, he left town the night I was leaving and told me to take whatever I wanted. I knew I could have cleaned out the house and left not a stick behind. He would have said nothing. Maybe that's why I left the house we had built quite intact. Having decided that I wasn't taking anything, I sat down and in the most organized manner wrote out a home-building list which had the bare minimum for me to begin my survival.

A big thing to tackle was food. I have a thing with food. I love good food, it makes me feel great and I salivate over gourmet cuisine. But I can't cook to save my life. I'm almost like a critic that way, can't do but can judge. I could be in the worst mood ever and all you'd have to do is feed me spare ribs or a steak medium rare – and that's it: I'm as happy as apple pie. I wondered sometimes if the Ex were a chef, whether I would have had the courage to divorce him.

The cook I had in 'our' house was fantastic. She was found after much sieving and searching. I hated to not have her. Luckily for me, she offered to cook in my new house and didn't ask questions about why I'd moved next door.

During the course of that time, she did take unusual liberties. If the potatoes were over in the Ex's house, she'd take some from mine. If there was no sugar in my house, she'd happily help herself to the Ex's stock. When the Ex was sick, she'd dutifully tell me and I'd as dutifully send across his Crocin. There were a lot of things that were ferried to and fro, but the marriage-saving ingredient wasn't one of them. Yes, it was a strange time.

There were other things I had to carry with me when I left. Non-material things like one no-taking-shit meter, four huge bags full of self-love, as-much-courage-as-I-can-carry, one happiness-pill-for-emergencies, 24x7-hours-of-hope and a small dose of reality.

It took me around four days to get my house adjusted into a state fit for the living and a small lifetime for me to adjust to my new status. That first night that I slept on my futon with my fairy lights twinkling, I felt confident and optimistic about the future. The worst was over. At least now my happiness depended only on one person – me; and from previous experience I knew this was a person who would never, ever let me down.

My Lean Mean Household Objects List

- *One bed, two chairs of which one is extremely comfortable, the kind in which you can slump all day, and a writing table*
- *Fridge, gas/microwave and mixer-grinder. I didn't have a washing machine as my kind, kind maid had offered to wash my clothes*
- *Four bed sheets and pillow covers, one for every week*
- *A set of cheerful curtains at which I stared a lot*
- *Fairy lights. They made me happy*
- *A vase for fresh flowers. The joy of making fresh flowers a ritual is therapeutic*
- *Broom, dust-pan, the bathroom's brush-broom-mat, mop cloth, stick-mop, mosquito-killer, a bunch of square pieces of cloth, for dusting, wiping, stuffing into the mouths of annoying people, etc.*
- *A shoe-rack, for there will always be more shoes*
- *A book-shelf — on hire. It was a gorgeous teakwood, which could fit my 1000 odd books (this could be anything that houses your passion; don't give up on the things you love, you'll need them when the person you loved fails you)*
- *A small photograph of my parents (or anybody else who truly loves you)*

This is all I needed to set up my house. Imagine the amount of unnecessary junk I used to fill up my home with.

My Survival Kitchen list

- 1 kg flour – to bake cakes because the house smells nice (if you don't have an oven, make it in a pressure cooker, it's worth it)
- 1 kg each: rice, wheat, toor dal, salt, onion, tomatoes, potatoes
- Chilli, turmeric, coriander, fennel powder, ghee, oil, butter
- Cold cuts (yum and easy), veggies (about 1/4 kg was sufficient for me)
- Tea, coffee, sugar, milk (the wake-me-up magic potion after those sleepless nights)
- Mustard, cumin, cardamom, fenugreek, clove, bay leaf, cinnamon
- Four spoons, forks, plates, glasses (why four? Well, it's cheaper than six)
- Two good whisky/beer/wine glasses depending on your poison. Two tea mugs
- Knowing how to cook a lemon pasta (Googled it); it's unbelievable how easy it is to make this
- One very good cook (on the other hand, if cooking makes you hum, it's a wonderful, soothing thing to do as you find your place on planet divorce.)

Chinese Whispers

My new house was beautiful and I was getting used to it. My next problem was who to tell and what. At this stage, it was still a separation. I didn't want to tell too many people about it for in case we got back together, I didn't want people to see the cracks when they saw us. Our good friends already knew, but over a lifetime you collect a host of acquaintances and other motley beings who randomly intersect as you walk through life, poking their inquisitive, cheerful claws into what's happening in your personal space. As I was slowly weeding through my list and preparing my lies, I got an email from a schoolmate. She was going to be in town and it would great to catch up after all these tumbling years.

I remembered the happy times we had shared in school. In fact, when I read her email, I could imagine her voice framing that cocooned world of happiness before adulthood hit me. I didn't tell her about my status in my reply.

I picked her up from the airport and it was reassuring to see that her goofy grin had remained intact, though her hairy caterpillar eyebrows were now beautifully shaped. We spent the evening together. I told her I was separated and she didn't ask any more questions. We spoke about a decade of dating, working and finding ourselves. It was beautiful. Whatever fear, discomfort and bugs-crawling-in-the-tummy that I felt about saying that I was separated had dissolved. It was the first time I had said it to someone 'not in the loop' and it truly wasn't so bad. I had made a desert storm out of a grain of sand.

I don't understand why I had this schoolgirl complex about the separation/divorce. Like I was the bad girl. Over time this would disappear, but I'll never forget her kindness and the open-hearted way she heard what I thought was my most frightful secret. After that it got easier. It's true, the more number of times you speak aloud about something that frightens you, the less power it has.

I went about telling my relatives and other family members. Now, I come from a large, rambling, very much involved-in-your-life, loving family. My rule of thumb here was simple. Tell the cousins, not their parents. It was a good strategy: the cousins gave me support without moralizing. They were young enough to respect privacy and didn't try to barge in and fix something.

Telling my friends proved to be more difficult. The close ones already knew; the rest were a mixed bag. Friends who think they are close to you but are actually not, friends you meet once a year and have a great time, friends from your staying-awake-till-six-a.m. days who claim to have a right over your life, friends from ex-offices, friends from may-I-borrow-a-pen encounters, friends at the sabzi shop – if you look at it, the number of people you meet is alarming.

I gave up, exhausted at the list. What could I say? We are living apart to see if we can live together? We are so unsure of our love that we have decided to test it with distance? We can't resolve our problems under one roof so we think if we stay under two roofs they'll go away? Silence was infinitely easier.

Naturally, the rumours began spreading. I learnt about them much later and laughed my heart out. Here are a few wonderful stories from over-imaginative gossips:

She didn't want to have children and he did, so they broke up. A version of this was one featuring an illegitimate child. I think people watch too many movies and television.

She is in love with B (a mutual friend who began spending a lot of time with me) and wants to marry him.

He couldn't handle the fact that she couldn't cook any longer. (Hmmmm.)

He was having an affair at office (yes, with work).

Their mothers fought and now the children have got dragged into the mess. (What!)

She is a night person and he is a morning person, so when one is awake the other is asleep. (We should have bought a single bed.)

And the ugly one:

The Ex was an alcoholic who was hitting me. This one was particularly cruel for the Ex would never harm a fly, literally. He used to blow mosquitoes off and anybody who knew him knew this.

I began living in denial. When the unimportant people asked me about the Ex, the standard reply was, 'He's fine, he's at work'. This pretty much covered his absence and his general state of being. Curiosity satisfied, nobody thought about asking more than that.

The important people, of course, couldn't be brushed aside. Like my boss. I told her what was happening for two reasons. One was that she was a good friend; the second was that I couldn't judge how the emotional upheaval would affect my efficiency at work. In case I was under-performing or was moody, I needed her to understand why and cover for me. I was losing a husband, I couldn't afford to lose a job too.

This helped. She wasn't a gossip and when I needed leave to meet the lawyer, courts, etc., I could take it without much fuss.

I had to tell so many 'good' friends about the latest in my life that I perfected the art of breaking the news. The first thing I said was: I don't want to discuss it. I didn't want to talk about what happened and the whys. This was how my life was now. Most people would respect that. A few pushy, inquisitive ones would badger me. Depending on my mood, I'd either tell them or yell at them. Those people, at least for me, quickly became personae non gratae. Though I understood that they came from a corner of concern, I didn't like being bullied to speak about my life. Through this mess, I found I had started seeking gentler souls, those who were genuinely warm and nice.

That is one of the biggest lessons the separation and the divorce taught me. To figure out what kind of friends I wanted to have. To understand who is important and who is not. Before, being an extrovert, I'd never spend too much time with the gentle, quiet souls. I'd hanker after the witty, interesting, twisted and crazy people. I still like those people, they are a lot of fun, but I now know with gentleness there is a soothing feeling of being loved: an uncomplicated emotional intelligence that turned the other way when I licked my wounds, but stood guard, sentinels in the shadows.

Crying over Spilt Coffee

When two people sulk, it is impossible to have a conversation. We were officially separated without a guide map about what to do next. I suggested that we meet every Wednesday and talk. It was perhaps the worst of my hare-brained ideas.

The first two Wednesdays, we met at a coffee shop. No need for the mist of alcohol in these clear-headed discussions. Once there, we sat and looked at each other, at the walls, at other customers and at that same old frappe menu for hours. I'm sure both of us can recite that menu backwards.

The problem was that I was the garrulous one, who could put her problems in a Power Point format with clauses A, B and C. The Ex was the silent one and he was going out of his way to prove it. I have never felt much violence against a single individual but when he sat across me, like this stubborn schoolboy, deep brown eyes tearing up in silence, I'd want to whack his ear. At least I'd hear an 'ouch'. I restrained myself saying that the point of these meetings was not to fight.

On the third Wednesday, he said, 'F*** it, let's go for a beer.' Most gratefully I agreed, for I was dreading another mental session of 'why-can't-he-f***ing-open-his-mouth-and-say-something'. We went to our favourite open air restaurant, looking over the sea. As we watched the masts of stationary boats sway in the wind, we spoke about nothing important. It was one of the best evenings both of us had had with each other in the last year.

We went back home. Then I bounced off the walls. I couldn't figure what to do. This creature was refusing to talk or deal with the problem. His escapism was pissing me off and this was killing any form of reconciliation. I didn't want to hang out with my Ex and have a beer with him. That wasn't supposed to be the point of our meeting. As I stormed and stewed in my house, I got a message from him. His mother was coming next week for a few days. At this point, he wasn't ready to share our marital problems with his family. With a heavy heart, I messaged back that I'd be there.

We had already decided that if any of his relatives were coming, we'd play husband-wife and not let them in on the truth, for doing that would mean the whole family would know. The Ex's mother was a gentle old lady. Completely non-interfering and a great cook, and we breezed through that visit. She did ask me once why I looked stressed. I told her it was work pressure. She smiled and told me that at my age I should be having baby pressure and not work pressure. Of course, a bouncy, whining baby to compete with the silent, sulking husband. I held my tongue and smiled.

This visit taught me something. I knew I'd never ever be able to play out this charade again. We couldn't live the lie. Again, I tried talking to the Ex and he said that he didn't have anything to say and that's why he wasn't talking. His mind was messed up and he needed space to clear his head.

I didn't have a choice, what could I do? I scrapped the

Wednesday visits and told him that he should call me when he wanted to talk.

He called me four times. All four times we had beer, discussed politics, books and life in the city. A vague, disconnected dialogue that didn't speak of love or regret or hurt or anything to do with 'us'.

There was no talk about the five years we had spent together, the crumbling of everything decent in our relationship, or the hope of rebuilding what we once had. It was like sitting and talking to a ghost who had come to reminisce about a world he no longer inhabited.

During those times, I never cried in front of him. I like my ego that way. I'd go home and bawl or suffer in the deepest silence, unable to comprehend this world I was living in.

For me, it was simple. If there was a problem, let's fix it. If we can't fix it, let's move on. This twisted silence was what I wasn't getting. When you don't have access to someone's head with whom you have shared your heart and bed for five years, it is extremely disturbing.

I think his silence began severing our bonds neatly. The words got cut off, then the love, the concern, the desire to make it work and finally one day, the marriage stopped being in any form except the legal one.

Even today, I am allergic to that particular brand of coffee shops. When I walk into one of them, I see our splattered silence on the walls, across the menus, filling the air with unhappiness and the severed reality that our marriage became. Luckily for the brand, only I can see this gory picture or they'd soon be out of business.

For something to work out, it requires two people. It's such a simple, commonsensical statement but at that time I didn't see it. I kept pushing, trying, wheedling, coaxing, whining, pretending to understand and even listening to that damn silence. Nothing worked. But life, that tenacious monster who sought out the best in the worst situation for me, did. It told me that his silence was a gift for me. What his silence did was push me further away from him and this, in a sense, made the final break easier. For when someone stops being in your life, how do you miss them? You mostly miss the concept of them and I very early on understood this. I let his ghost go and his living presence stopped troubling me.

Is Kissing During Separation Cheating?

The point of a separation is, as any well-meaning sensible person will inform you, to see if you can live without each other. The distance is supposed to bring perspective. You are encouraged during this time to date, go out, have a life and not sit at home and pine. That, in theory, sounded beautiful to me. I had done enough pining for a lifetime. Or two.

I was getting used to things like lifting a gas cylinder alone, ordering for one, so-that's-how-the-electricity-office-looks, I-have-to-pay-the-full-rent-all-by-myself, carrying home the groceries and building my upper-arm strength, when a friend called and said that she'd like me to meet someone.

Incidentally, he was separated too and she thought it was a good 'oppoturnitee' for the two 'separtees' (sounds like amputees) to meet. I couldn't think of a single logical reason to refuse, so I agreed to see the 'separtee' in one of my favourite restaurants. It had a jukebox, cold beer, great food and a nice boho ambience. No matter what he turned out to be, the evening wouldn't be a total waste.

I was on time, he was ten minutes late, a gentle boy who didn't understand what to do with his separation. I spent the evening consoling him. She was his first love, first date, first everything and obviously she hadn't taught him a thing. After he spent two hours telling me how miserable he was, I could see her point. I have a feeling he didn't realize that we were on a date, and that he was supposed to make me feel good. Luckily for me, the beer did its job but much to my horror, I found myself making snide remarks about his sorrow. I quickly asked for the bill, and quoting work, escaped. He paid and I didn't insist on going Dutch. I called it 'shrink' fees.

The next day, I confronted my friend asking why she had forced this 'pile of sorrow' down my throat. She was most apologetic. She didn't realize he would make our meeting a moaning-about-the-ex session.

I met the guy again a couple of years later at the same friend's party. He was now divorced and a serial dater. He gushed about how much confidence that meeting with me had given him. Oh no, the poor, poor women, I thought.

As for me, I wasn't looking at dating someone. I was too busy working, getting adjusted to my new life and enjoying being alone. Then I met a guy who I would have been normally attracted to in my single days. Thick wavy hair, worn to the shoulders, supremely confident about his place in the world, he was all that and more. All my 'all that', that is. He was a liberal, a bleeding heart, liked dogs, single malt, music, sang like a dream and was so funny. I think he liked me too.

He was somebody I met at a workshop, one of those creative theatre artistes. It had been so long since I had even met an interesting human being and here was this gorgeous breath of fresh air. We went out three times, mostly with other people, but I think the attraction was there. He knew I was single but wasn't aware about the separated bit.

Every time I met him, I felt the dilemma, bubbling and boiling, urging me to spill the truth. What could I have told him? Technically, I wasn't single, I was legally married.

Could I say, 'Let me play with your heart for a bit and make up my mind which man I want to be with? I am married but trust me, this isn't cheating. You're my experiment and you will help me decide whether my marriage is worth saving. If you're a bad kisser, I'm going to march right back to my husband'.

What strange, strange problems a divorce throws up.

He kept asking me out and I would go with a swish of skirts and hair in a braid. I wasn't having an affair but it felt like it. One night, we had gone to the other side of the city to a random party, after which we headed to his place. I didn't mind as there was another girl too. I thought she'd be protection enough as I made up my mind and tried to find my way through this particularly murky wood.

That girl (who I am never going to hire as a watchman), the minute we got to his place, went somewhere inside and slept off. I started panicking. I knew he was going to try and take our simmering attraction to the next level. He started by changing the music to something soft and cosy. A part of me was thinking, I am so old, I know exactly what the moves of this dance are. Instead of sitting opposite me, he sat next to me and a slow hand began making its way up my back. I knew the minute it reached my neck, he'd turn my head and kiss me.

As his hand progressed, I kept thinking whether I wanted to kiss him. It had been five years since I had kissed another boy.

Not just that. I still couldn't decide whether I wanted to. As the hand reached my neck, I blurted out the most stupid statement that held the biggest complication. 'I am married,' I said. Oh. The hand fell and a stony, hurt silence descended between us.

I spent the next ten minutes explaining my situation. I apologized for I knew I had led him on. He spat out a 'don't say sorry' and told me he really liked me. Hell, so did I, but I couldn't. The way I am made, I can't be tied to one man and explore the possibility of another. By then, dawn was breaking and I took a cab back home. In that yellow and black mule, I became completely miserable. That theatre guy was almost perfect and I had blown it for I didn't see a possible, even a temporary, future for us. I decided I wouldn't date during the separation. I couldn't do it. I was someone who hated deception. This whole staying apart was tough as it was; I couldn't complicate it by messing up my inner core beliefs.

A man wasn't like a job. I didn't have to get one to leave one. I didn't want to get into that absurd logic of 'see the kind of men who are available and then decide' or 'see if you can handle being alone'. The reason to be with the Ex had to be that I wanted to be with the Ex and not that I didn't want to be alone or I wasn't meeting anyone nice. That guy, though he doesn't know it, brought a lot of clarity into my life.

That day I was miserable and I missed the theatre guy's smile like a phantom pain in my gut. The morning chill of that ride stayed with me for almost a week, reminding me again and again what a mess life was.

The Happiness of Aloneness

It was the Ex who caused the separation, but I think I was the one who loved it. It was such a relief to step into my space, where I could give free rein to the storms in me without wondering about their effect on the other person.

The first two months, a part of my head would miss the Ex but the other part began celebrating other things. It was almost like being reborn, there were so many things I started doing. Like:

Going alone to a restaurant I liked, ordering myself a beer and a pizza, looking out at the street as it emptied, and crawling home, hugely satisfied with the evening and the company.

Inviting friends home. I had prided myself on having a happy, warm home filled with books, beer, single malts and good food. The last one year, the unhappiness between me and my Ex had hung on the floor like a carpet of sorrow, which I'm sure every single visitor sensed when they entered the house we had shared.

I started taking care of myself. Walks, pedicures, manicures, haircuts. Sometimes when the inside is not feeling that good, you don't care a damn for the outside.

I started doing the things I had stopped doing with him. No matter what anybody says, when two people get together, some things die a natural death. Things that only one person is passionate about, which the other person doesn't give a damn for or doesn't get. Listening to a particular band as the other person can't stand it. Or food that one person is allergic to. It's not a bad thing, just a behavioural thing.

Like a maniac I started attending plays, music festivals and all those culture-vulture things my liberal arts soul craved. I'd see something in the paper and get up and go. I didn't have to check whether someone else's timetable was free. I didn't have to beg, plead and sell how much fun Chau dancers from Orissa would be. I didn't have to stew angrily outside a venue waiting for a certain person. It was so great to be alone and go performance-hopping.

I stopped doing things halfway. When you are deeply unhappy, life is a halfway effort. There is no joy in anything that is done. When I was living in that gloom of 'our crumbling house', no matter what happened, the gloom would suck me in. A surprise gift from my mum would inspire a weak smile and I'd step back into the stony, inert silence that the smile had escaped from.

Looking back, I have no idea how I had survived that house. I am not normally an unhappy person. I like being cheerful, full of sunshiny happiness. The situation was such that the listless drudge of status quo shrouded everything. It was a place where nothing survived – hope, laughter, happiness, fun – anything good in life. I am amazed by how I managed to get away, for the grip of unhappiness is a vicious one.

The new house helped a lot. Not seeing him made me realize I didn't need him. I was even beginning to suspect whether I loved him at all. When someone puts you through a lot of hurt, it is difficult to think of them with a burning passion.

When I'd think of him, I'd keep thinking about why it happened, how he let it happen, how we did this to ourselves. It was difficult to touch the happiness with which we had gotten married.

My solution for this was simple. I stopped or forced myself to stop thinking of him during the day. I actually had a time. After 9 p.m. I could think about him. Cleverly, I stayed out at this time, distracting my mind. When I come back home tired, I'd think of him. But when your body is exhausted, there is only that much the mind can suffer.

I think if the Ex and I hadn't had such a lousy time together, this separation would have been too horrible to bear. The truth was that I began finding myself again and there was no room for anyone else. Even a husband.

The separation brought me a sense of freedom I had never ever had before. In my life, I have always been surrounded by people. I remember once in college, I had snuck out to the cinema alone. I was hugely excited and wondered how it would affect my viewing experience. Small-town Bangalore had other plans. Immediately, a friend's friend's cousin saw me and 'rescued' me by asking some stranger to swap seats. My protestations were brushed aside. She probably thought the poor thing had nobody to go to a movie with.

After that, boyfriends, friends, family would trot along for any movie or restaurant experience, and slowly I forgot that I craved solitude. Being separated in a big city like Bombay helped a lot.

Busy, bustling Bombay, with its 12.5 million plus souls trudging around finding their happiness, had no time for me. If I went for a movie alone and saw a colleague there, she'd shrug her shoulder and perhaps mutter, 'She was weird anyway'. Or if I met someone in a restaurant, they'd merely wave. Very rarely did anybody join me. It was the unwritten code of this grand old city made up of seven islands to allow a person their privacy, in spite of the fact that over 20,000 people dotted per square kilometre of it.

This lack of involvement was what I needed when I was learning how to survive. By being tough and not mollycoddling me, Bombay taught me to stand on my own feet. Its gritty, no-nonsense world forced me to stop stumbling and pushed me to start walking – towards a freedom I knew I carried in my heart.

III

THE LONG MANICURED HANDS OF LAW

The Wicked Witch Who Will Turn the Ex into a Pumpkin

I had never stepped into a lawyer's office all my life. This doesn't just prove what an exemplary law-abiding life I had led but it is also testimony to the fact that I had neither invested in property nor been fortunate enough to receive an overnight, unbelievable inheritance.

The time had come for me to break that record. Being a lawyer-office virgin wouldn't help me navigate the world of divorce. I was a bit shy about asking my friends so I did what any stupid person does – I walked into an unknown office on the sidewalk lured by a lawyer's board displaying a trailing serpent of degrees behind the name. It was almost like I had wandered onto the set of a Hindi movie.

A pan-chewing, red lipped, buttons open till his waist, gold chains dangling from his wrist, black hair sprouting out of ears caricature belched loudly as I entered. I was happy he had had a good lunch, but I wanted to get on with why I had walked in. Timidly, I squeaked that I was contemplating a divorce and I needed a lawyer to represent me. Rubbing his hands he said, 'Ophcourse, ophcourse, it's modern time, we are liberal.' I had no clue what he meant but thinking maybe he knew his lawyer business better than his English, I spoke about how I was looking for a mutual consent divorce.

He wanted the details. 'Why? No sex? Sex with other lady?' I dematerialized, fast. He managed to give me his card though and, as red spit darts flew my way, told me to contact him anytime, day ... or night. He'd give me an 'especial' rate, because I looked 'yung and unknowing of real-world'.

I learnt my lesson: no more walking into random offices, for you never knew who lay in there waiting for the unsuspecting being-in-distress. I agonized about who to call and finally after adequate squirming picked a few friends chosen for their discretion and contacts. They gave me some numbers and I called the first lady on the list. Her secretary set up an appointment and I was soon ushered into a plush office. I wondered if my bill would pay for that cooing, helpful secretary's next outfit and matching accessories (including, I kid you not, an orange six-inch heel).

After listening to classical music, going through a Cosmopolitan (surprised they didn't offer to 'do' my nails), I got called into a largish boardroom. A woman lawyer floated out. How do I explain her? She was wearing a saree like a suit, but her hair was loose and wavy, her perfume strong and her matching jewellery crisp.

She came up to me and instead of shaking hands, clutched my tiny palm in her red talons, looked deep into my eyes and gushed that she was so sorry that I had to come to her office, but we have to bite the bullet and address reality. She bit her 'bite' as she spoke. I noticed that she wore green kajal to match her saree. She was a specimen I wasn't exposed to. I was used to the women of the dark dens I inhabit, who wore jeans and had a scruffy, let's-talk-Sylvia air.

We sat down after ordering me a 'nice, hot, strong, cup of coff-ae' (every word enunciated without breaking eye contact, I was just glad that I didn't start blinking maniacally to counter the Kaa-from-*Jungle-Book* stare). She continued, 'Men are such bastards.' I hate this sort of sexist remark. She didn't know my story and I didn't want her making a judgement about my Ex. It seems silly to be protective about a man who practically jumped up and down on my happily-ever-after dreams but this wasn't only about him. I felt like she was playing me.

She knew I was hurting and she thought that by bashing the 'enemy' she'd win me over. It didn't seem very fair or humane. Luckily for me, the phone rang and I told the surprised Vodafone executive that I'd come over immediately.

I blurted out that I had to rush, there was an emergency. Not to be outdone, she cooed that if she could help with the emergency, she'd be glad to. I smiled bleakly and staggered out of her clutches forever. Before I left, the six-inch orange wonder gave me a bill of three grand. I was furious, but before I could break their beautiful glass vase, the lady materialized again and smiling kindly said that this one was on the house. Umm, what exactly did I get free?

That evening I was telling the Ex what horrible lawyers I had met, when he casually said that a mutual friend of ours had recommended someone. He had met her and she was 'Cool'. If I didn't mind, he'd ask if she'd represent both of us, since it was anyway a mutual consent divorce.

I thought about it for two seconds and agreed. We didn't have kids, property or pets to divide. There was nothing I stood to lose except for a marriage and that was lost. I agreed and we decided to meet her the next day.

We walked into her office and there she sat. The first lawyer who looked like you and me. She wasn't a freak, she listened to us, told us politely what we were in for. It was such a relief. We were spinning into abnormal, crazy territory with our emotions here and I wanted a lawyer who wouldn't add to the angst. Someone who was basically decent, nice and kind. By a miracle of luck we had found her.

Later that evening, I was updating a good friend about how I had found this friendly, 'good-vibes-giving' lawyer and he began to panic. He said that having the same lawyer as my husband was foolish. All sorts of things could be put into the legal document and I, being such a gullible fool, would sign anything (he'd known me long enough).

He refused to listen to the fact that I had felt comfortable with the lawyer and the Ex wasn't an evil person, he was just someone who couldn't make a relationship work. He said a few rude things about the Ex and hung up promising to call back with a solution for a problem I didn't have.

Promptly, the next day his 'rescue' call came. He had unearthed a lawyer. She was good, very pro women's rights. I could completely trust her as she was a friend's friend and had been briefed on the whole thing. He said that even if I decided to go with the Ex's lawyer, I should run the documents by her.

My situation was that of Alice in Wonderland and I was taking whatever experience was being hurled at me, with a pinch of humour and zero fight. I though this way I could ride the tide. I breezily agreed, one lawyer, two lawyers, four, what's the big deal? I was still going to get a divorce. I gave her a call and as the conversation unfolded, both of us realized much to our amusement that she was the same lawyer the Ex had hired. We had a good laugh and she said rude things about my friend, which I gleefully repeated back to him. She wasn't on anybody's side and dealt with our case in a professional and compassionate way.

When the divorce came through finally, the only pain we suffered was the one we had meted out to ourselves. The lawyer was someone who was in the background holding our papers safe, as my tears flowed unchecked and he stared angrily at the wall, standing together, yet a little apart, one last time.

Chatting with Pickpockets and Others

Courts don't look like they do in the Hindi movies. There is no banister, no wigs and no 'Mai Lord'. Just as I had never been to a lawyer's office, I had never been to court (duh, that would be logical or maybe not considering the hundreds that go unrepresented in India). They should have school court-visits, where kids glimpse where they have to go for justice in their country. Maybe this will get our courts to polish up and not look like a refugee camp of souls who have lost all hope.

The Ex was also a court-virgin and we decided to go together. We were the kind who asked the lawyer what to wear to court. She said we could wear anything semi-formal that didn't draw attention. We dressed formally. I wore a cotton kurta and the Ex a full-sleeved blue shirt. Then, like frightened children, we took a taxi and made the one-hour ride, each one looking out of the window, contemplating the host of thoughts that such a situation merits.

At the end of the ride, I asked him what he was thinking about. He said that he was thinking of our happy times. I felt like such a twerp: I was thinking of our horrible times. Gulping down the feeling that I may not be such a positive, healthy human being, we marched in.

The court was a multi-storeyed building and being early birds who lost the worm, we decided to wait for our lawyer on the ground floor. The Ex and I spent an hour there wondering why all the to-be divorcees were men and why they looked so unwashed. As far as we knew, being gay in India was illegal. When we saw one of them being led in handcuffs, we began to suspect that something was amiss. The Ex spoke to the guy next to him. He was a pickpocket he said but he'd come to support his brother who was a thief with a possible conviction hanging over his robbing head. The information was handed out casually, as if we were talking about how the standards of *vada pav*, a Bombay-special street food, had fallen over the years.

He asked us why we were here. When the Ex told him about the divorce he got very theatrical. He stood up and almost started screaming in Bombaiya Hindi, much to our embarrassment, that the only good thing the world had was 'luv' and we must not kill our 'luv' but save it. People around stared, salivating with curiosity. Entertainment, finally! The Ex smiled politely at the pickpocket and immediately called the lawyer. We were redirected to another building. We had come to the criminal court instead of the civil one. Thank god, for I was beginning to wonder whether after the divorce I'd start looking like these guys.

The floor above seemed much more like a divorce court. Lots of couples strewn around, an odd child or two. It was a crummy place. One of the saddest, most disheartening and gloomy places I have had the misfortune to be a part of. Every couple was a tragedy. There is obviously nothing happy about coming to get legal sanction for something you broke. It was a place of ruptured dreams, broken-hearted regret, manipulative emotions and you sensed that anything good and decent had been thrown out of the window. It smelt of unhappiness.

The Ex and I moved closer to each other. We were getting a divorce but we had nothing in common with any of the people there. We saw a woman who obviously had been very beautiful in her youth tell an overweight man, with yellow teeth, 'What should I do, commit suicide?' and then burst into tears, while he looked the other way, banging a ham-like fist into a peeling plaster wall.

A little child was showing the lawyer his report card and his mother was saying, 'That man disturbs him all the time. Look at his marks, they are so low.' That man was a small, nondescript person. He held out a puny hand, which had a few bones jutting out, touched his son's shoulder and pathetically implored, 'I don't disturb you, right?' The son shrugged his father's hand off with an impatient frown and looked at his mum and the lawyer. Three against one.

There was an old couple. The father could barely walk and would shuffle every half hour to the guard to ask something. They had come with their young daughter who seemed grief-stricken. Her eyes were vacant like she had had a lot of drugs. The couple was filled with misery and resignation. They made a tiny, wretched bundle of humanity, hardly taking up any room on the bench.

Another woman threw money at a man's face, screaming that she didn't want his money, and stormed off. The man bent down quietly, picked up the notes with his lawyer, as the rest of us watched. He stood up with the bundle of now messily gathered currency in his hands and looked around the room, unsure of what to do next.

Another man held his hand up and threatened to hit his wife in public. A lawyer immediately stepped in between them.

It was perversely fascinating. I'm sure if we had filmed how those people were acting and showed it to them, they would have been very embarrassed at how badly they had behaved.

The Ex and I had never felt so normal in our lives or so grateful that we were able to go through this with our dignity and, I think, our basic human goodness intact. We sat on the bench and people-watched, squirming at this humanity we belonged to, till we were called. Every day innumerable dramas would be enacted here as emotions splintered and I wondered whether the walls were sick and tired of this excess.

The lawyer had already warned me that the judge would ask us to go for counselling. It lasted one session and the lady who took it was politely uninterested. She asked me why we couldn't be together. Unable to think of anything, I said that he was always at work. Then she probed whether he had given back my gold. Somehow I knew the answer to that one wasn't 'What gold?' and I said 'Yes' as seriously as her. Later, it was explained to me that this was done to protect the wife. How wonderful our legal system is sometimes. I thought of a woman, probably abused by her husband and forced into a divorce. She may have no lawyer if she had no access to such privileges. Just when she thought everything was lost, a legal third party would ask her 'Have you got back your gold?' That gold, which was wrongly denied to her, would be given back and she'd buy her freedom with it. I'm sure I'm overdramatizing but it felt good to know that there was someone watching over women. Men? Don't know.

Our first day in court was done. We now had to wait six months for the final divorce. The whole experience had been harrowing. These places are far removed from our everyday reality and nobody warns you how bad it will be. It was a world of broken people and their shepherds.

The Ex and I headed for a much needed beer and biryani. As the sun set, we toasted each other. We were warriors who had returned intact from The Land of the Dark.

Forget about the Money, Honey

The divorce was going to become a reality in six months. A few friends of mine, urgently, carefully and with great tact began dropping words: 'alimony', 'he owes you', 'maintenance'. I squirmed. This mention of money to compensate for the loss of love seemed very tacky. They had uttered these things before, but there was a six month deadline and if I didn't ask for it now, I'd have to forever hold my silence.

How could I ask him for money when both of us had lost so much?

I had lost five years of my life. Years where I should have settled down, bought a house, had kids and done the things any regular middle-class person did. But so had he. Those five years weren't coming back to either of us.

He had hurt my love, battered my confidence, caused me immense pain and through a stupid misjudgement on his part, frittered away the future we were carving out. That didn't give me the right to punish him. I knew he was unhappy and making him pay a 'fine' for causing me unhappiness seemed to trivialize what he had caused. Maybe, secretly I didn't want him to have the pleasure of giving me money to assuage his guilt.

How do you do the math for five years of living? It's not like you keep tabs on who bought more potatoes. What do you measure this time with? How much does a year of your life cost? No matter what he gives me, he can never give me my twenties again. He can never give me the belief in the permanence of marriage. He can never compensate for those two years of complete darkness and pain, where there was not even the hope of light.

He had changed me for life. Given me life skills I never knew I had. Forced me to learn how to combat a mammoth depression and emerge triumphant. Kicked me into the adult world, so that I'd put my fists up and defend every bit of my happiness, even at the cost of drawing blood.

He had taught me the language of unhappiness.

I had to relearn things – to trust again, to believe in goodness, to not be bitter, to smile, to have fun, to not let my self-worth be dependent on the capricious nature of love, to start dreaming of a future. I had to relearn to live.

My normalcy had been shattered and I had to painfully reconstruct it again. Do the cracks show? I can never tell. All I can hope for is that if they do, they are not ugly. That they look like badges of courage, war wounds and not bitter infections poisoning me from the inside.

I sometimes wonder if he has any idea of what he caused, but I quickly castrate this thought and I tell myself that it is his journey. Now that we are apart, I have to learn to think only of myself. I shouldn't care whether he's learnt his life lessons or about his emotional maturity. I survived him. Whether he had survived me was his business. In the worst of times, I'd feel like a toy broken by a petulant child.

I sat down one day and calculated the cost of the things I had bought in 'our' house. I had got the pretty things – the ones that weren't utilitarian; the quirky things that made a house a home – the soul-fillers of brick and mortar constructions. I had paid in part for the bigger things – the fridge (I remember us arguing and buying the bigger one as it was supposed to last us at least half a lifetime, and the television (same logic). In fact, we had bought the best and biggest of everything, thinking that since we were spending on a lifetime of togetherness, we shouldn't short-change ourselves.

I looked at the figure. It wasn't much but it could finance a holiday in Brazil. Wistfully, I thought that instead of getting married if I had gone on that holiday, I would have saved time, money and heartache. I tore up the figure and threw it away. Making him pay half the bill for this house we built was too painful to navigate and what kind of a payback was this?

The intangible price of five years was humungous: the men I didn't marry to marry him, the jobs I didn't take to be together, the friends I lost to be his friend. The precious, priceless trust he broke on a whim. The pain he caused my parents. The fear he left in my heart, about being alone, about love leaving you anytime.

He had hardened my heart so much that I had to work on it, thawing it gently over time, through logic, philosophy and faith, so that I began feeling like a human again. Yes, he could give me the money, but he could never give me back the intangibles.

My mother said that she would like to give back the gold his family had given. He refused to take it saying it was mine to keep. I didn't insist. 'Gold for a rainy day'. The money we jointly owned was split into two, without any discussion on who put in how much.

I have a feeling we were so civilized about the whole thing for we didn't have much to lose. These weren't large numbers we were talking about. There wasn't that much to make us greedy enough to shred our well-mannered selves.

I refused alimony simply because I was working. I was privileged enough to have an education and a job. I didn't need what he had. I have mostly been an impractical person, but I think I handled the finances of my divorce practically, sensibly and fairly. For me, this was the right thing to do. It was, in fact, the only thing to do.

Broken by a Hammer

Half a year passed quite uneventfully. We met a few times but nothing of consequence happened. Our conversations went in loops. Nothing could be done until he took care of the 'Big Problem'. He was having trouble doing that and I couldn't help him with it. For a lot of couples, these six months are just a waiting period where nothing more can be done to save the marriage. A minuscule part of us was delusional enough to think that it wasn't over till the last minute. I think neither of us wanted to accept the inevitable, till it actually happened.

It was one of the most frustrating periods in my life, when my happiness was dependent on another person. What made it worse was that I couldn't do anything about it, but had to helplessly wait, while he wrestled with his demons (and as far as I could make out, the demons were going to have an easy win).

The failure of our marriage was imminent and one day, quietly without a bang, it was the date of our final court appearance. This time, the Ex and I didn't have to have a consultation about what to wear. The mood was very sombre, like we were going to a funeral. In a sense we were – it was the death of our love, hope and marriage.

We entered the court and found a list pasted of the couples who had a hearing that day. I read their names and wondered about their stories. Then we panicked; our names weren't on the list. Quick calls to the lawyer and once again we were informed that we were at the wrong place, this time the wrong floor. An optimist would have seen this as a sign not to break-up. We were realists.

We climbed up one floor and the strong stench of urine hit us. It felt fitting. A place which ends things should smell like this. Like all the goodness has gone and only what's most foul remains. This time we were too wired to people-watch. I think both of us were aware that at any point now, we could still say, 'Let's forget it' and walk back home, together.

It felt like we were suffocating this last chance we would ever have, deliberately and cruelly. I looked at him and wondered what was on his mind. His eyes filled up and he shook his head, helplessly and bleakly. I think it was one of the worst days of our lives. The wait without hope.

As we waited, the Ex held my hand. I'm not sure if we are the only married couple who held hands in a divorce court, but I do know we are one of the few to do so. I understood. I was also his friend. It was a mute sorry, a clutch of pain, a solidarity in hurt and love, all rolled into one.

I didn't hold back his hand. I had begun teaching myself to be alone. I didn't want to be his friend anymore and I didn't want to understand. The worst part is, a part of me knew I could and, over the years, after that nightmarish day, in my quieter moments, I found that if I thought of him as a human being and not 'my husband', it became easier to digest what had happened.

The lawyer sensed our mood and kept a distance. She was sensitive that way, giving us our privacy in a roomful of people, and I was glad we had decided to go with her. The man at the door that led to the judge's chamber announced our names.

It rang loudly, gaudily, vulgarly in the room and felt eerily unreal. Like the walking dead, the Ex and I got up and went towards the judge. We stood in front of her. It felt like I was going to be expelled from school because I had done something very, very bad. My heart was thumping, my skin went cold and my chewing gum got stuck to the roof of my mouth. It was frightening. I think the Ex wanted to reach out and hold my hand again. I moved a little away, hastily.

We looked at the judge and I wondered what she looked back at. Did she see two young people who could still make it work but were throwing it away on a whim? Or did she see two entirely mismatched humans who'd never stood a chance in the first place? I'd never know.

Then, like in all good books and movies, an interruption happened. Here we were, with baited breath awaiting the final stage in our grand story and there was an ad break. It was so annoying.

Suddenly, a woman interrupted 'our' moment, placed around five velvet jewellery cases in front of the judge and said that she didn't want 'his charity' and the court could do whatever they wanted with it. Then she turned around and walked out before anybody could react. The judge immediately sent a clerk after her. They couldn't find her and the cases lay there, staring at the Ex and me, now mute participants in our own drama. I was itching to open them and see what was inside.

The court had to decide what to do, for they couldn't leave them like that. The judge eventually gave them to a women's rights organisation and asked the clerk to get a receipt for the sale of the jewellery. All the while, the Ex and I stood patiently in suspended disbelief. Our lives were going to change forever and here they were deciding what to do with random trinkets that had no connection to us whatsoever.

I was thinking that if this was any other service, I would have lost my temper and demanded that my case be attended to first. However, here I stood, meek as a lamb, head bowed, awaiting judgement, for the sword to flash and my head to roll.

The judge finally looked at us. I almost wept with relief. Then she asked in a booming voice, whether we wished to end this marriage. The Ex, I cannot believe it, said nothing even though she was looking at him. My clear voice rang out, 'Yes'. As her eyes shifted to me, he mumbled an affirmation, which I don't think she heard.

The judge stared at me and I held her look. Hey eyes again went back to the Ex and this time he muttered a muted 'Yes' with a quick half-nod of the head. She took her small gavel and banged it on the table. You could hardly hear the thud but it was the loudest blow to our lives. Firmly, she announced, 'I now pronounce this marriage dissolved.'

IV

WHAT BREAKS WHEN THINGS SMASH

The Cat's Out of the Briefcase

My office was a safety zone. I was one of those lucky few who worked in a zero politics, fun office. I had moved from agency to corporate and I found the transition soothing. The people weren't as crazy and wild as the agency crowd but they were lovely individuals who were good, decent, kind and humane beings. They never got into your head, mucked around with your core in order to understand the 'inner you'. There was no debilitating angst about 'what am I doing with my life, I need to be an artist in Venice'. Everybody was aware and comfortable with the fact that coming to work was an act that paid their bills.

They were, I think, slightly conservative people. While furious whispers about X having an affair with Q did do the rounds, I never heard any sexual innuendoes, saw fatal attraction undercurrents or even quietly 'peaced-out' behaviour like a reefer smoker.

Everyone was married, had children and, I presumed, lovely homes filled with normalcy. Of course, as I journey further through this life, I realize nobody has normalcy. Everybody attempts to achieve it with some of them being more successful in showcasing it. At that time, however, I was vulnerable, anxious and felt that I was a person with a dirty secret, a shameful past.

It was relatively easy to put on this still-married farce for we never socialized much with each other and even if we did, it was never with families. Nobody had seen the Ex to enquire about him. Neither did they move with the same social set who knew our story. Only my boss knew and she kept secrets.

I could have continued my entire stint there without anybody ever discovering my status if it wasn't for this lovely green bottle, which apparently had found its maturity and raison d'être in France.

Yes, wine had always been my Achilles heel. With whisky, rum and beer, I knew my limit and if I chose, I could stop before the happy-high became a rambling-drunk. Wine was a mutating creature. Every bottle differed in strength – how it hit you, when it hit you, who you hit, etc.

These tortured grapes were my lethal poison and I have innumerable tales in my life dedicated to it. Luckily, I don't remember most of them. And fortunately for me, the stories happened only when good friends were around. That's why I'm not a deck-hand on a shady vessel sailing to Corsica. Or a belly dancer in Saudi Arabia. Or a stuffed human parrot in the private amusement park of a yesteryear rock star.

My previous escapades should have been warning enough but like all creatures who enjoy a good time, I conveniently forgot and happily floated into a wine drinking session with the colleagues.

It all began when one of our office friends was gifted four bottles of premium wine and he wanted to make a night of it with the team. My house was the closest, so everybody trooped there with much excitement. On the way, we bought expensive cheese which smelt like tiny, furry animals dead for a week. None of us were wine connoisseurs but we were very much intrigued about how something that cost one-tenth our salary would taste.

I wasn't too worried about exposing my status for the 'husband' was 'at work'. The evening began. It was beautiful and relaxed. As a group, we never spoke about intimate stuff but only about things that happened in office, the world, music, movies, etc.

I come from a planet of intense friendships, where when we meet, we get right down to the bottom of everything that is troubling us and dig out the worms and the sunshine in each other. This casual hanging-out was new and alien. I appreciated it, this ease of companionship without intimacy.

As the bottle level got lower and lower, our tongues got looser and looser. Soon we were sliding into, yes, the never-before visited personal territory. Love stories of the past began being swapped, office crushes were confessed, and bitter enmity was spat out.

Funny, bizarre details emerged. One of them had a single ovary and was worried whether she would be able to have children when she got married (in the time it took me to get over the divorce and write this book, she had a child). We assured her with drunk confidence, as she got a bit teary-eyed about her nether regions, that nobody could tell she didn't have a second ovary and you needed only one to make the child. One of them confessed that he hated his job and was saving up to build a hotel in his hometown. I never even knew the guy could cook. He promised to bring me his special mean mutton curry the next week. Ugly secrets of abuse were cocooned by the wine and gently allowed to float into the open, in tiny spirals of sadness. How could I remain silent?

I felt that I had the biggest secret stuck in my throat, waiting eagerly to break free. I exploded with my words, which tumbled out one after another, revealing bare facts of my current situation and I apologized for keeping them in the dark. They were awesome. My super boss immediately said they didn't have to know about it as it was not part of my work. Another colleague shushed him. With wine-confidence, he demanded the gory details. I obliged, feeling lighter and lighter as I spoke.

Know the best thing about that evening? The next day nobody spoke about it. Not a single one of them held my hand and squeezed it saying in that overtly considerate tone, which used to make me cringe, about how they felt my pain and were with me, etc. Work was back to normal, inefficiently normal I must say, for each one of us had the biggest hangover imported from France. I was amazed at their decency and intuitive collective wisdom which refused to talk about drunk-night disclosures. Slowly, I got used to it – my secret that everybody knew and kept.

The year and a half I spent there were critical to my moving on after the divorce. My non-judgemental wonderful workplace paid the bills for my survival and gave me my first public space as a divorcee. The surprising bit was that it wasn't bad at all. I was just another corporate cog, who woke up every morning, put on my money-earning suit and headed to work. Correction. I was just another divorced corporate cog – the solo beaver whistling while building its dam.

I Didn't Break-up with You

A couple is a newly formed planet. When it explodes everything that made the planet gets destroyed with it. The people who floated into our orbit transmogrified into nothingness. His friends, Her friends, Our friends became 'Who' friends? His family disappeared into the mist, like they'd never existed in the first place.

Associations and cross-associations shattered as if struck with a heavy sword. There are no overlaps in this. The break is clean. Each human piece goes back to the place where it started, before it knew me or him or us. All the people bits rewind frantically and by doing so make it seem that the recent history never happened – I never met them, they never met me, the Ex and I never came together and merged our worlds to form a new one.

The unfortunate part is that there were a lot of people who I really liked, who had to give me up. Call it the collateral damage of divorce. What hurts is I wonder how they could ignore the connections which were made. Isn't there any other way to navigate this understandably blurry path of loyalties? Was my whole worth based on being a connection of the Ex? The answer to this is an undebatable no, but I suspect these disconnections were done simply because it was convenient.

Nobody is comfortable with murkiness and I mustn't blame them for choosing the easier option. This chapter is a tribute to those people who disappeared from my life but who still claim a place in my heart.

The Old Man Who Sold Books

The Ex had introduced me to him. A bookseller who loved the Ex for he thought the Ex had an eye for good books. Widely travelled, the first question this nonagenarian would ask anybody who met him was, 'So what do you read?'

In our first meeting, he understood my taste in reading. In our second, he gave me free books – Ted Hughes, Doris Lessing, a few one-off Booker winners and a humungous Ogden Nash. I still have the books but I haven't visited him. I have no idea what to tell him and, I have a feeling, he'll have no idea what to tell me. I am uncomfortably conscious of the fact that I may not have a claim to those free books, which I got by association. And I know without a doubt that he liked the Ex more.

The Ex's Brother

Being an only child who sorely missed siblings, marriage was a chance to get that brother my mother refused to produce in spite of frequent pleadings. I really liked and looked up to his brother. He was warm, funny and lovely. Tolerant of my eccentricities, I believe he liked the person I was and was glad his brother had found me. The last meeting I had with him was when he told me to leave the Ex as nothing 'could be done'. That's it. What could one say, after everything had been spoken? And broken.

His Friends Who I Liked, My Friends He Liked

All of them dissolved into thin air. Everybody picked a side, in spite of us explaining we weren't warring. People were blocked from Facebook, numbers were deleted and birthdays were ignored. I picture this as a scene of carnage, where the two sparring kingdoms return to their individual countries, leaving in the centre a pile of dead bodies, friendships, affections and good times. All forgotten and turned to dust.

Our First House

It was the place where both of us played house-house for the first time. This was before we moved into the 'big house' of the break-up. It was the home that introduced us to the magic of Bombay, where we discovered each other and decided to marry. It was the place where our teenage dreams came true. Painted doors, wild parties, books strewn, beer and other intoxicants in the fridge, the lift which wouldn't work, and some deliciously unforgettable moments when we thought life couldn't get any better. After we had shifted out as most upwardly mobile couples do, we'd often go back and look at this place, with nostalgia and love.

After the divorce, I've never gone back. The Ex called me one day out of the blue sounding equally blue. He said he had passed the gates of our old house and had broken down in the cab. I didn't know what to say. It was like a killer missing the victim he had murdered.

The Aunty Who Wanted to Adopt Us

Every migrant will have a story about a local person who took them under their wing and fed them copious amounts of homemade food. Ours was a headstrong sixty-year-old, who would keep her husband quiet with a single 'Hoy!' or that's what she claimed. She had been married to him for forty-five years and he would sit in a corner silently, an invisible man further faded out by her booming voice. Her sister once told me that when they were very young, this man was a tyrant. A wife-beater. I couldn't believe that the meek man who tried to blend in with the wall, once had the rage that could raise a fist to this feisty woman.

She had worked hard her entire life in an office, and bought property when Bombay real estate had zeroes you could count and not figures used to describe the distance to the moon. She was childless and her fascination with the 'south Indian couple' was childlike. If she could, I'm sure she would dress us up in our traditional costumes and keep us in her showpiece cabinet.

This doesn't undermine her innate kindness and boundless generosity. From getting us two gas connections to homemade remedies when we were sick, she was our champion cheerleader as we meandered through the living practicality of life in Bombay. When I told her we had split up, her eyes filled with tears and her sorrow washed over me, bringing with it that familiar feeling of failure.

There are a lot more of them, some too painful to mention. When I think of everything that transpired, a divorce is another birth, where you have to wipe clean yesterday's slate. It is not for the faint-hearted but only for those who are very desperate and have no other option.

Once the deed is done, a new planet will be rebuilt. That is the nature of life. Perhaps, in my old age I will feel richer for these experiences and will be the grand old dame who has been there and done that. Though, right now, on some days, all I can still feel is a faint bitterness that has lost its sting but retains its presence.

Annoying Aunties and Other Mosquitoes

There is a moral cretin in each one of us and some of us give it more freedom than necessary. A divorce has a way of bringing out the purists, the holier-than-thouists, the tsk-tsking ugly faces of false concern. I was subject to a fair share of them. Luckily for me, none were people I was close to. This helped for I could easily brush off their offensiveness like a particularly nasty bug which had landed on my shoulder. I wish I could have squished these bugs into non-existence but I think that may be a crime.

Somebody's somebody's mother's sister, one day, called me saying that we had met once and she had heard about the divorce. She launched into why I should go back to the Ex, and even though the divorce was legal, it still wasn't too late! I just didn't get it.

First of all, why is this woman, whose face I can barely recall, so interested in my life? Why does she insist on giving me advice that is guaranteed to make me unhappy? How can she possibly think that being a silent doormat is a better fate than the one I am carving out? And lastly, why do I have to listen to her politely? I didn't. I told her in excruciating detail exactly what an interfering pain in the butt she was and forced her to hang up. I doubt she will make a call like this again. And if she does, it definitely won't be to me.

However, she was just the beginning of the do-gooders. I was shocked by the number of people who were trying to save my marriage even after it was over. Maybe the television soaps weren't very interesting at that time. In the beginning, I would rage against these people who would tell me to work it out, that I could still go back. I would want to yell, 'You moron, if I could work it out, why did I get a divorce in the first place?' I regret I never yelled this out, but any such encounter would drain me, leaving behind only a furious desire to run away to a land where there were no people.

Over time I developed my strategy. I would listen to what they had to say, politely and seriously. Then I would look deep into their eyes and say, 'Thank you for talking to me. It really makes a difference.' These prigs would be thrilled with what they thought was their good-deed-for-the-day. They'd walk off, brimming with the milk of human kindness, which was actually curdling. As soon as they disappeared, I would develop amnesia. Forget about them, and never meet them again.

Some people, when they heard of the divorce were cruel and downright insulting. The annoying part is that while they were being so, they thought they were doing something righteous. They were doing me a favour by being mean to me. They actually had the notion that all I needed was a stern talk and like an obedient child I would fix my life. Fighting was no use. 'Reading too many books', 'Western education' – these were the arguments that would surface. Of late, I am convinced that the best thing to do when you're faced with an idiot is to ignore him or her. It is possibly the worst insult you can give any human being – don't acknowledge their existence. These days when I have to talk about my divorce, I am careful about the way I word it. By making the argument about me and my decisions, by centring it on the indisputable 'I', I enter a zone which cannot be questioned.

A few of my divorced friends think it's important to have discussions, to initiate dialogue so people understand. I differ. Dialogues can happen only when people are willing to listen. Moralists have only one viewpoint – theirs. People don't realize that the mildest of insults are chiselled in stone when you are going through a divorce. The whole process is already a volatile, highly vulnerable one. In such a scenario, any act of cruelty is magnified and causes undue hurt. Like what a fourth removed aunt of mine did. She was a doctor, the wife of an officer high up in the Air Force. On the outside, she was immaculately dressed and sparkly but on the inside she was an uncivilized louse. When I told her I was divorced, she said, and I kid you not, 'So soon!'. I smiled my polite smile and stopped myself from elaborating on the extensive time-frame my relationship had. Then she blurted, 'I always thought this would happen to you.' Next, this bumbling b*t*h of insensitivity barked out questions, asking for details. For the first time in my life, I informed someone it wasn't any of her business and I didn't want to discuss it. Now, every time I look at her, all I can remember are those unkind words, 'So soon'.

Here's another example of an equally tacky human being. He was a far-off somebody (now a nobody in my books), who had come to my parents' place when I was there. He started a tirade about how my mum had walked on coals to raise me (trust me she didn't, she took a car, bus or taxi like everybody else) and demanded to know whether this was how I repaid her kindness. What did he mean? I was getting a divorce to deliberately cause my mother pain? By staying in an unworkable marriage I would be doing my mother a favour? Why didn't he get it that in this whole thing, the person who suffered the most was me?

How could he even think that I was morally obliged to be unhappy for the rest of my life to please my parents? They'd hate it. Luckily for me, my dad spoke up. He categorically told him that they were not in any pain or unhappy that I had got a divorce. He stressed, on the contrary, that they were extremely happy I had freed myself from such an unworthy association. That shut him up, but I knew I was lucky.

There are countless voices out there who blame us for being happy, for taking these irrevocable steps to ensure we are okay. Words like 'selfish', 'irresponsible', 'headstrong' are hurled at us.

I think this is because they are afraid. We are the ones who have stepped out of the neatly drawn nasty boxes of society and they are scared others will follow suit.

In a society like ours, 'happiness' is considered a dangerous thing – something that shouldn't be indulged in; something that has the potential to ruin you. While on the other hand, endurance, stoicism and suffering are applauded and cited as examples to follow.

Ask any person on earth whether they want to be happy or unhappy and the answer would unsurprisingly always be the same. If that is so, then why should anybody stop themselves from chasing the happiness they deserve? I didn't and that will always make me happy, no matter what happens.

Why is Everybody Around a Couple?

I never realized all my friends were couples till I became single. Then, everywhere I looked, my friends flocked in twos. They were a few solo cruisers but they were an exception and currently faraway.

While before it was perfectly normal to hang out with my couple friends, it now became painful. Every time I saw these twosomes and looked at their dual interaction, I would wonder how they managed to keep it together. How they avoided the slippery slope of divorce? It's not as if I could ask them, 'Have you guys ever thought of a divorce?' That kind of thing is not done, especially by a divorcee. I would also see a few obviously mismatched couples, miserable with each other and wonder why they didn't end it. At that time, I didn't have the wisdom to realize that people choose the lesser evil. For me, the lesser evil was going away, for them it was staying.

The other reason I hated being with a couple was that it made me feel bone-achingly, pathetically, snivellingly lonely. A cold, anxious heaviness would settle in my heart, because I didn't have the foggiest idea of how I would survive alone. I wasn't a well-oiled team anymore. Nobody would pick a paneer piece off my plate (the extra-browned bit I found yuck), or if I ordered soup I couldn't command someone to share half of it. I would have to ask, to request, to enquire.

Friends began dropping me home, picking me up. Luckily, because I stayed in one of the safest cities in India, I put a stop to that. However, there have been innumerable times when I've caught a cab at 3 a.m. and my poor couple-friends have stayed up till I reached home and messaged them. I got to messaging 'Reached home safe' when I was just halfway home. At 3 a.m., nobody calculates time and distance accurately. I remembered during the five years I was with the Ex, nobody would worry about me or what time I crawled home. It is true, when you are a couple, people tend to worry less about you. I guess they think the worrying should be done by the other half. When you are single, however, you can be everybody's problem child.

Couples do innumerable, insignificant things together every day. And when you get divorced, you miss each and every one of them. Those initial days, my single status would burn into my skin and I would miss the ease of couplehood in the most trivial situations. In a restaurant if I ran out of money, I would have to 'borrow' from a friend and not delve into my partner's wallet and tell him to pay my share without a second thought.

I couldn't afford to feel more depressed than I already was, so I stopped meeting my couple friends. I started looking out for new single people. I found lots and lots of them and it was liberating. My favourite of that bunch were the ones who chose to remain single and would, with the zeal of someone preaching a religion, tell me how magnificent singlehood is. The singles who were single because they hadn't found that special person were not as attractive, for the only problem in their life was that they didn't have a partner and every opportunity they would get, they would mourn this fact.

Here was I, who had left behind a seemingly normal, functioning man. Occasionally, I would want to set up one of these 'I-need-a-man' obsess-ers with the Ex. I never did, probably because I didn't like any of them that much. The other good part of the singles' club was when I called them up to go out, they didn't have to 'check' with the other half whether they were free. Like me, they could make split-second solo decisions.

The single-by-choice people were my teachers. The way they did things, who they were, how they celebrated their freedom and most importantly, that unshakable, heady confidence in themselves, were things I coveted and worked hard to get. It was as if I had connected with my college group of feminists and was inspired and fired up again.

I didn't have to listen to MIL/FIL/DIL (Mother-in-Law, Father-in-Law, Dog-in-Law) problems. It wasn't that I had become unsympathetic; but confidences of this nature would leave me feeling cold. I remember skipping a friend's tenth-year wedding anniversary not because I didn't wish her well but because I, perhaps quite mean-spiritedly, didn't want to toast to the institution of marriage.

I was sore and needed time to get back to being normal. I don't think anybody who is in coupledom gets this. After my experience, if a friend of mine is going through a break-up, I would visit her alone. I would give her my solo time. I would not ask her to do a happy couple thingamajig with us.

The funny part is during this time a very close couple friend of mine asked me to come home saying it was important.

Dragging my feet, I landed up only to be faced by a deluge of complaints they had against each other.

It was exhausting to say the least. Fortunately, I had a clarity about their problem that only an outsider gets. I spent hours explaining, deconstructing and finally through logic showing them why their marriage was working and this, what they were going through, was only an adjustment issue.

They had to listen to me. I spoke the truth and they had enough intelligence (at least, it was bigger than their ego). Eventually, they saw I was right. Even today, they thank me for keeping them together. Imagine a divorcee who fixes marital problems. How had I turned into that?

Word got around and soon random people began calling me up with 'What should I do?' questions. For a spell, I helped out; I had to, these were people I cared about. Then, as suddenly as it started, the calls stopped and I had to step down from my role. Maybe I was so good that everybody was happy now! I must confess, though, I missed playing the Agony Aunt for these phone calls kept the loneliness away.

It took me almost a year to not be acutely affected by other couples. Six months of it were spent in isolation, but I realize in retrospect that's not enough. The only way to get over couple-envy is by going out there and hanging out with them. Finally, that day did come, without me realizing it, when a couple was just another set of human beings. Not a bitter reminder of what I had lost.

After my marriage broke up, I re-learnt how to be single. How to take pride in that status and feel good about it. It wasn't hard for it's a great way to be. I remember one particular family dinner, where my aunt fought with her husband, my mum fought with my dad and my cousin fought with his wife. I was the only one not fighting with anybody and enjoying the delicious Kerala mutton stew and appam, diplomatically ignoring the gathering dark clouds.

My sixty-eight-year-old aunt seeing my happy little bubble amidst this smoke and fire, said wistfully, 'I wish I was like you'. I grinned. I would have laughed out, but it wasn't polite. I had finally got to this place. Everybody around was a couple, but now that was their problem.

V

GOING CRAZY ONE DAY AT A TIME

Wandering Everywhere with a Hankie

Sometimes I think the process of getting a divorce, going through it and its aftermath should be called Boohoo times. I have never cried so much in my life.

Anything could be a trigger.

Spotting the pani puri-man, who had been pronounced the best after a complete survey of a five-kilometre radius over two years – it had involved much research and nuanced debate. Not just that, spotting the Ex at said pani puri stall was even worse. The last thing you want to see when you are broken of heart is the guy who broke it stuffing a pani puri into his face.

Passing the goldfish we had christened Dob Bylan in the pet shop window.

Hearing a lame joke he owned, cracked by somebody else.

Coming across orange juice in a supermarket (I hated it, he loved it). The weird part is through the separation I drank a lot of it. These days without coercion, by choice, I ask for it. Who knew a divorce changes the palate?

Spotting a shoulder in a crowd encased in a familiar shirt. Don't worry, I hadn't slid to that place where I chased that shoulder through crowds and threw myself on it, demanding to be loved.

Hearing a radio ad that would have had us in splits.

And sometimes, even things that didn't have a particular, deep, poignant meaning – a horn, a footpath, a shadow whose only job was to prove the existence of the sun at noon. On some days, without reason, without warning, everything would trigger a brine festival.

Work was especially a fertile crying ground. A colleague only had to say, 'My husband', and my eyes, annoyingly, without rationale, would fill up with tears. I would quickly excuse myself and go to the loo for a good bawl. Luckily, I wear contacts and I got adept at rubbing my eyes furiously during these moments and saying 'My contacts are troubling me'. At one point, my contacts 'troubled' me so much that a colleague recommended I change my lens brand.

These weeping sessions could start even in the middle of a mood of happiness. I would return home after a perfectly great day and start crying, and I would cry my heart out. Gigantic sobs would wreck my body. After hours of downpour, I would lie emptied of everything in me, sniffling pathetically, waiting for the dawn.

I must say that during these extreme moments of sorrow, which mostly hit at night, daybreak would bring relief. With the first rays of the sun, I would fall asleep to wake up a couple of hours later and get ready to work without the trace of a tear.

I used to cry a lot in cabs too. There was something about being alone in the backseat, about seeing the city that had seen the courtship and breakdown of my relationship, pass by in a soothing eating-up of miles, which would turn on the tap. I think Bombay cabbies are so used to people crying in their seats that they respect a person's privacy. Not one ever referred to my tears when I paid him later.

I began using so many tissues, I started dreaming of the trees that were cut to keep up with my crying. It felt terribly irresponsible and unfair to those mute barks that grew towards the sun unselfishly. Why should the earth pay the price of my sorrow? Not crying was not an option as I didn't have control over it. The solution hit me when I saw a brightly scrubbed schoolgirl with a handkerchief pinned on her uniform.

I had found my eco-friendly tear wiper – the good old hankie, used by children and very old ladies who crochet. I started carrying them in my handbag. After the third standard, I think this was the first time I had one of these white square pieces, slightly starched and so bloody unhip.

I went out of my way to find pretty ones, the kinds a granny would covet. The place I stayed in was an old colony filled with stores nobody would visit but manned by faithful shopkeepers who looked as ancient as their businesses. When I told them what I wanted, without a change of expression, they dived down and unearthed crumbling boxes. Clouds of dust would part and reveal beautiful, painstakingly made hankies with borders, slight oddities, dashes of colour. With that single prop I could have starred in any period drama. It was worth the trouble to find these places as I wanted the quality of my tear-mopper to be at par with the quality of the tears.

An old Parsi lady in one of the shops I visited was so thrilled I had asked for a handkerchief, she dashed into her house (which was attached to the back of the shop) and brought out an imported cookie tin older than our independence. From its deep recesses emerged heartbreakingly beautiful, embroidered white handkerchiefs. She confessed she had stitched them herself. For forty-five bucks, they were an unimaginable bargain.

How my friends ragged me. They were, I think, shocked when they saw these little lace-bordered squares in my purse. One of them, who was extremely concerned, even asked, 'You're not losing it, are you?' I grinned maniacally. 'See, I'm happy but I adore hankies.' I liked ironing them and feeling their warmth, knowing that soon they'd soak in salt water and become damp, cold, rolled-up balls, testimony to another day of pain.

While this deluge of tears was flooding my life, I would remind myself that what I was going through was very tough and tears never harmed anybody. I felt lucky to be able to cry so much. I know a lot of people who held their tears in, suffering in their closed grief, never letting it out. Whenever I would speak to them, they'd say they wished they could cry but I would see the barely hidden pride in their inability to shed a tear. I do not know which is better. I think each individual has a survival mechanism in them. Mine told me the tears were washing the Ex away from me. With every bout of crying, he was fading like that curry stain on my top.

As usual, the mechanism was right. There came a day when the tears dried up. I think my reassurances to myself, about the normalcy of these crazy bouts, was an act of extraordinary kindness to myself. I would allow myself to go completely ballistic without freaking out. One day, surely, these irrational leaks would stop. And they did.

I never spoke about my breakdowns to anybody, so the only one who was worried about this behaviour of mine was me. It allowed me the space to not think of the crying as a big problem. If I had told my mum or my friends, they would have started working overtime to fix it. They would have sent shrinks, reiki, prasad from pujas, self-help books and other 'helpful' things to block this release. Not one them would have thought, 'This crying is good, let it run its course'.

A friend of mine once asked me how I knew what to do for I did have incredible clarity about how to fix myself. I replied quite honestly that I didn't. Perhaps I was like this hurt animal who knew exactly which herb to eat in a forest of a gazillion plants to heal its wound. I just knew what I knew and I listened to myself more than anybody. It worked. My body and mind came together and helped me get back on my feet.

When the tears stopped it wasn't like I was completely okay. I think I did hurt for a long time after that. In the frequent inner melodramatic moment that would pop up, I would think the hurt was chiselled into my eyes, little flecks of sorrow. I would peer and peer into the mirror to spot the bruising of the soul, but I looked the same. I guess real life is always more ordinary than the extraordinary pathos we feel inside.

Playing Stalker-Stalker

Ever wanted to know what the person who hurt you the most is up to? I never suspected I had a masochistic voyeur in me. Or that I would walk into a private space uninvited. The divorce had come through, everything was supposed to have been done and dusted. It felt that way for three months and then one day, I woke up and began obsessing about the Ex.

These feelings popped up with an intensity I couldn't ignore, triggered off by finding the key to the house we had shared. I had forgotten to give it back and it never struck the Ex to ask for it.

I couldn't avoid its presence. It stared at me, yelling and screaming, asking me to do what good, serious stalkers do. Walk through the apartment when the owner wasn't there. I didn't even try to resist it, though I was fully aware it wasn't the right thing to do.

I bunked work and set off to his apartment, for I knew he would have dutifully gone to office. If he had decided to bunk too, I would say I had forgotten my socks which was incongruous enough to be plausible. Knowing my memory, he wouldn't be surprised. I was sure he would not demand to know why I was walking into his house again. He was too gentle and well-mannered for that. Unlike thieves, there was no fear of being discovered.

The key turned with a click and the house smelled of nobody being there. It had a quiet, empty silence. I walked around and saw that nothing had been changed. My interior decoration touches were still intact. I didn't know whether this was because I was a fabulous home decorator or because the Ex was too lazy to change anything. I suspected the latter.

As I wandered through the house, I looked at objects and remembered where they had come from. The living room had the flat long pot with grass in it, which was supposed to be our 'lawn' in Bombay, the antique green lamp that claimed to be precious jade, which was meant to bring good fortune (bah!), the huge cupboard filled with books (a birthday gift for he had wanted a bookshelf with doors), the straw mats I had bought from an old woman on a trek, the bolsters we had carried on our heads as a joke from the market, the empty spaces from which I had taken my share of the objets d'art, every corner spoke of our life. How did he live here?

The bedroom unkindly had the pillow covers that I liked and he didn't, for he found them too loud. I wondered whether he remembered how much he had protested when I had bought them. There were tickets of a concert we had gone to that I had stuck on the bathroom door. They were still there, pasted pitiably, dead pieces of paper. I couldn't help myself and tore them off, leaving the edges behind stuck under the cello-tape.

I remembered in the guest bedroom I had hidden a pair of silver earrings he had given me, for I didn't want to take them with me and I didn't want to give them back. I looked for them and they too were lying there undisturbed. It was almost as if the Ex had preserved our life together without touching anything.

I knew if it had been me, I would have wiped away every trace of the previous occupant. I didn't want to analyse what this meant, but like a true stalker, once my curiosity was satisfied, I wanted to explore more and violate the space completely.

I lay down on the bed and held my breath. Nothing happened. I ran my hand over the bed sheet and thought about how naive the sheet was. The people who owned it had changed so much, but it lay there, sparkling in its colours, looking joyful in the sun.

For the first time in my life, in that house I felt like a guest, an intruder, a defiler of somebody's sacred space. I couldn't wait to get home and I ran out. His house was no more mine.

I went back there six more times. The third time, I opened the wardrobe and wore his shirts and felt very sorry for myself, for us. They reached down to my knee and the long arms hid mine. The huge shirt made me feel very, very small. I sat in the extreme corner of the bed, taking almost no space and hugged myself with his empty sleeves.

It was getting dangerous. I was getting addicted to walking through his empty house and remembering our times together. When I was staying there, these objects didn't have any power. Suddenly, they were all I could think of. They began invading my dreams, digging up the most insignificant memories, clogging my 'moving-on' efforts.

I don't know how long this would have continued if it weren't for the fact that the sixth time I was there, I heard a click and the Ex walked in. I looked at him and lied effortlessly. I told him I had come to look for a pair of socks, which I thought I had left behind in the laundry.

He nodded as if it was the most natural thing to do after a divorce – come looking for socks – and asked me to stay for tea. I thanked my stars I wasn't wearing his shirt. As we sipped tea, I handed him the key. It felt dangerous to hold on to it anymore. He looked surprised and asked me to keep it. He said I could come anytime and use the place. Trying not to sound too sarcastic, I told him I had my own house.

I don't understand why he looked hurt. He always did when I would say these practical things. We were divorced now. Was refusing the key insensitive on my part? Or was he the crazy one, who wanted to keep the doors open? It didn't matter. As he took my key, my stalker dreams broke into a million fragments. It felt like a thing that had not happened at all, a thing that I did not do in real life. My unforgivable behaviour of visiting his house, walking through its doors and reliving the stories of the objects I had chosen to make a house a home seemed unreal. As unreal as my marriage.

Hypochondria and Other Diseases

Work takes the edge off our loneliness. I would wake up in the morning and have somewhere to go to, every day. Except weekends. As a new divorcee who wasn't in a relationship, a weekend was fraught with peril. I didn't want to go out with my friends (one of the reasons being a serious paucity of money) but staying in meant being completely, achingly lonely.

At some point during that time, one Friday night, when I refused an invitation to go out for a drink, I suddenly began feeling sick. A fever crept into me and started wrecking my spirit.

I began feeling tired and my voice got that hollow quiver sicklings have. When family and friends called, I groaned and muttered about 'being too tired to talk'. Immediately SMSs to go to the doctor, home remedies, what to eat, what to avoid poured forth. The advice to go to a doctor was immediately junked as I am petrified of these people in their white coats. Going alone was not an option.

The Ex and my mother offered to take me. I weakly waved away their kindness. I felt brave, I was battling this gigantic monster on my own. I stayed in bed, the cook kindly made me soup and then Monday morning arrived.

My fever vanished. I wore my clothes and skipped to work. The next Friday, the fever returned, an uninvited visitor bringing with it the delicious comfort of being able to disconnect from the world. I caved in and stayed wrapped up in the blanket, 'weakly' reading my book.

After around eight such weekends, people started to get genuinely concerned. Blood tests were advised; a friend stormed into the house and said we are going to the doctor NOW. I protested. I knew if I told the doctor that my fever was a weekend visitor, he'd tell me what I already knew but didn't want to acknowledge – the fever was psychosomatic. And everybody would know what a hypochondriac I was. I didn't want to lose their sympathy and I didn't want to get better. For being better would mean I would have to start looking happy and that was such an effort at this point. With 'high fever' I could look as miserable as I felt inside.

When the anxiety about me reached such a high pitch that it became threatening (they were talking about getting a doctor home), my fever vanished and never came back. Before anybody could give a sigh of relief, the next weekend, the stomach upset made its presence felt.

I am the kind of person who drinks water anywhere and eats anything. A number of childhood years spent running away from my father's watchful eyes and giving hawkers a livelihood had made my stomach tough, with a cast iron lining that could conquer even the most unhygienic of edible things. I have eaten roadside mangoes with fiery red masala, corn liberally coated with a vile green paste, unidentifiable species of animals fried in carts, which were suspiciously called 'chicken', brown, murky beef pieces that didn't taste like beef. These delicious banned food-meats had tumbled into my stomach quite merrily. When various other co-eaters had groaned the next day, claiming to be dying, I was fit and fine, ready to gobble fluorescent red kebabs from the new entrant down the road.

Suddenly, my constitution seemed to be breaking down. I would get a stomach upset eating bread. Again, I would battle diarrhoea alone, drinking down bottles of ORS prepared by the kind cook. The only disadvantage of this illness was that the cook refused to make me good food. She'd make bland, insipid stuff and claim that it would help my stomach.

I wasn't that heartbroken. Mutton samosas, biryanis, kebabs with roti, green chilli keema, *farscha* and *paya* soup were all on speed dial. As soon as the cook left, I would order nourishment for my sick self.

The upset stomach phase didn't last very long and, ironically, I suspect it was because of the 'speed-dial delicacies' I used to feed myself. I soon reached a point when I couldn't have outside food and wanted the delicious meals I used to get at home. The upset stomach had to go and it did.

The throat infection was the next one in queue. This was fun. I could drink fine brandy with cinnamon, cloves, cardamom and pepper, and sound very, very sexy, as though smooth stone pebbles gurgled in my throat emitting a gravelly, smoky tone.

My voice would purr out into the phone or when people dropped by to visit. They would advise me in a concerned manner to not have anything cold and leave behind lozenges. This phase went on till my throat genuinely began to hurt. Maybe the effort to produce the gravelly tone had begun to scratch my boom box. My body got frightened of an imaginary illness turning real and quickly developed a back pain to give the throat a rest.

Finally, this illness seemed a good one. I had hit the jackpot in hypochondria. I didn't have to take medicine, I could eat good food, I was not forced to go to a doctor and anybody who knew anything about it told me to take lots and lots of rest. Yay!

That's exactly what I did. I used to get into my bed on a Friday night and not leave the spot till Monday arrived. Friends got me books, flowers, treats. It was great. I finally had a bona fide illness that wasn't an uncomfortable one to pretend to have.

It was the most convenient excuse to disengage. I didn't want this space to neatly slash my veins in parallel lines. I just needed something people could file away in their heads as a legitimate reason for me not turning up at their parties and dancing on their tables (what's wrong with dancing on raised surfaces, I say?).

Why didn't I speak the truth, and tell my loved ones that I needed a little time to myself before I went out again? My ego, which was already battle-weary and bruised, wanted to protect itself. This need to stay in bed couldn't come at the cost of my self-confidence. Somehow, the excuse of an illness was preferable to an excuse about the breakdown of a relationship. I hated to think of my acquaintances whispering at the parties I didn't go to, 'she is not here, been very upset after the divorce, poor thing', etc., etc. I wanted to show the world the illusion of my strength.

I Forgive Me

Three words everybody needs to chant over and over again during a divorce are 'I Forgive Me'. It's a crazy time, almost like war. In a sense, it is emotional warfare and what happens is such a twisted, vile knot of negativity that coming out of it with even half a smile is a miracle. The toll it takes on confidence, trust and love is unquantifiable. My behaviour during these times was not entirely palatable. In moments, and I am ashamed to say, it was insidious, devious, petty, dangerous and manipulative. It stemmed from the desperation of a cornered animal, who will do anything to survive. Anything. That's why I need to say this.

I Forgive Me For:

Making the Ex feel bad about things he didn't have control over. I took the one 'blame' as a springboard and multiplied it a thousand-fold to justify the claim to a divorce. It took me a while to realize that the one 'blame' was enough and I needn't have indulged in the entire laundry list of complaints.

Being an irrational manipulator and greedily claiming more than my share of love from people who were genuinely concerned. I asked and asked and asked and when they couldn't give anymore I felt hurt.

Vacillating. Saying 'Yes', saying 'No', saying 'Maybe' to buy time, when I should have been honest and given the answer I knew all along.

Emulating a hysterical banshee. Crying at opportune moments, using my tears and leveraging my womanhood to get additional sympathy. It took me a long time to understand that though the Ex didn't cry as much, he felt just as bad. And on some days worse.

Ignoring everybody else's pain and being self-centred in my unhappiness.

Changing into a tougher person, who is so fearless about consequences that my loved ones suffer, anxious about what I'll do next.

Chasing happiness tirelessly, fiercely, selfishly and proudly for I can't shake the belief I've earned the right to do so.

Walking out instead of staying (I believe this has to do with how I was brought up, the guilt of not making the marriage work.

My rational mind knows that some things can't be made to work, but my emotional self feels like I've let the family down).

Not keeping in touch with the Ex's mother, who was wonderful. I let her go as she had no place in my future. Like so many others, strings were cut, and relationships sacrificed to move on.

Being bitter, for spitting spite, for thinking dark, mean thoughts, for being uncharitable.

Deliberately not calling the Ex on his birthday, knowing it would hurt him. As time passed, we became desensitized to each other. I doubt he will feel bad if I miss a birthday now. Maybe he wouldn't even realize I didn't call.

Pretending I had gone through the worst of times. It was bad but I was not as victimized as someone who was physically abused or emotionally tortured by pure evil. The Ex, at the end of the day, was a confused, not a terrible person.

Not having the maturity to have dealt with the entire thing better (but it isn't like we have an Emily Post for 'the model behaviour while undergoing a divorce')

Painting myself as the 'good' person. Every side has two stories and to date I don't want to acknowledge his.

Being rude to the moralists, the preachers, the holier-than-thous who weren't harmful. They were merely uneducated about new-age dysfunctionality and had the sensibilities of terrorists in a peace procession. A more gracious way to react to them would have been not to react.

Causing my parents more pain than they ever thought they'd have to deal with. In a sense, you can't protect your parents from you. The inexhaustible love they have for their precious daughter is their biggest weakness and my biggest strength.

Turning into a person who doesn't care for what other people think. Who doesn't listen. Who will not be tied down by rules. Who will follow paths of her own making, no matter the cost.

Asking god to do mean things to the Ex. I have stopped (quite recently, I must add) and am grateful the powers that be didn't listen to my immature rants.

Being the kind of person who feels bad when I hear of someone getting a divorce. Not just that, I go out of my way and do everything in my power to save their marriage. (Why?)

Wearing my happiness on my sleeve, across my chest, painted in 142 point-font, every time I meet the Ex, so there is no way he can miss how much better off I am without him.

The nights I still cry. The pathetic, weak regression after having moved on.

The inability to be bothered by petty complaints and ignoring people who claim a portion of me by stating cloying please-love-me phrases – 'You never call', 'Why didn't you come for my birthday', 'Good friends don't forget my anniversary', 'You didn't meet me when you came to my side of town'. I have turned colder but more compassionate.

Waiting for too long before snapping the ties.

Becoming a more aggressive person, giving up the softer side of me, so that I won't get hurt again. I have clearly understood now that if I want to live my life in a particular way, I have to go out and get it. Nobody will do it for me. Nothing is gifted. Everything is taken.

Waiting in limbo. Waiting in unhappiness. Waiting in desperation. Praying for the miracle that never happened.

I Forgive Me all of it. The things I did and didn't do. The words I said and didn't say. The life I lived and didn't live.

I Forgive Me Everything. Anything. That Thing.

Write down your I Forgive Me list on the next page. Go ahead, write the worst. You will feel immensely relieved and the book won't judge. Neither will it tell anybody.

I Forgive Me For:

VI

THE MATHEMATICS OF LOVE

The Mangalsutra That Bought Me Freedom

A friend of mine joked that if I had spent as much time looking for the guy as I did for the wedding saree, I might have still been married to him. It's mind-boggling how much effort I had put into making the wedding day perfect. It was almost like a mania, everything had to be the way I envisioned beauty. Why is so much importance given to a single day, when the proof is unquestionable that the days that follow are more important? Philosophically, though, you can't be getting married thinking 'Who cares, it may anyway not last'. The only way you can do the whole shindig is by believing that this is truly the happiest day of your life. Ah, well.

The wedding saree shopping was a nightmare for my let's-not-wear-too-much-red-and-gold tastes. For some reason, every designer in India thinks a wedding saree is meant to be an overdose of beads, pearls, stones, gold, shimmer and shine, weighing a ton. I stomped in and out of shops, with my enthusiastic aunt and mum, trying on varied colourful, gaudy, loud, glittering outfits. At the end of the day, the only thing I took back home was a humungous headache and two old ladies, sick and tired of their picky progeny. How can those blushing brides walk wearing those things? Every time I draped one over my head, I felt like I was carrying a truck on my body.

The traditional sarees didn't have too many embellishments but in red and gold, they screamed their look-at-me-ness, their richness and their price tag. I finally found what I wanted in a small, non-fussy, traditional shop, which had been on its little plot for over a century. It was beautiful, muted with a non-paisley design.

The man who sold it to me was an old person who loved the art of saree making. He explained how this saree had been woven by hand with great care and actually had real gold threads. In fact, he told me the name of the village where it was woven and said that if I took this saree there, they would guide me to the weaver. It was awesome to have a saree that could meet its maker, whose roots I could trace back. Then, with a shrewd twinkle in his eye, the old man said that if ever I wanted to sell the saree, I'd still get half the value. I was impressed. A saree that was an investment. I bought it and it's with me, unlike the husband, wrapped in net, being saved for a rainy day, though I don't think I could wear it again.

I think my friend was right. I took more care to choose my saree than the man. That's how affairs of the heart work. They are more impulsive than the affairs of the wallet.

I looked for the wedding saree in three cities. I looked for the boy in one.

I went back to the saree shop seven times to convince myself that this was the one I wanted to wear. At the end of the third date, the Ex and I were a pair.

I took everybody's opinion on the saree, even went to the extent of clicking pictures of it and mailing them to my best friends. I never consulted anybody when I started going out with the Ex and I didn't care what anybody thought of him. I loved him and that was enough for him, for me. At that point, with the intense foolishness that a romance brings, I thought it was enough for our future too.

The second wedding object that consumed my passion for perfection was the *mangalsutra*, the sacred necklace that identifies a woman as married. Immortalized in Bollywood and in afternoon soaps of the theme 'women-are-doormats', it was an object that my friends and I had laughed and mocked at many a time. However, come the traditional wedding and I morphed into one of those women who wanted the chain around their neck to be the ultimate symbol of love. Not really, but I wanted it to be special, though I knew I'd never wear it more than two or three times.

I remember thinking intensely about what kind of chain I'd want, which would solemnize my marriage. I couldn't adapt the one my mum wore, for the Ex and I were from two different castes, speaking different mother tongues. I wanted a neutral design which wouldn't insult either family, as families tend to take these things seriously. I even looked up Jewish wedding symbols. After many unfruitful days, I hit on what I thought was a very creative solution. I decided to fuse the traditional mangalsutra design from each side and make an original, one of a kind piece.

It was to symbolize the coming together of two different entities to create a brand new one. Yes, one does get nauseating when one is getting married.

Now that this idea had taken birth in my mind, executing it proved to be more difficult than I had thought. I could never look at jewellery designing as a possible career option. So, I got a friend who designed advertising layouts to draw out exactly what I wanted. She was such a sweetheart, she even painted the design golden. Then began the long search for goldsmiths. You wouldn't believe how un-obliging they were.

Each one came up with his silly excuse – 'This design is impractical, it will break', 'God isn't depicted in this way', 'I can make you two mangalsutras, each one sticking to the traditional design', 'Marriage is a serious affair, don't play with the mangalsutra', 'If you find someone who will do this design, I will write my shop to his name'.

Phew!

Seeing how bad I was feeling, the Ex offered to make a cardboard cut-out of the design. I glowered. I should have realized then! In the end, I settled for an ugly, large gold chain, which had two lockets.

I never wore it after the wedding day. Its utility however lasted a long time. I almost understood why people gift gold. It's like giving a large cheque with the figures appreciating every year. The mangalsutra bailed me out twice.

The first time, I pledged it with the bank to get the money for the advance for my new house when I moved out. The irony doesn't escape me. The second time, my best friend needed urgent funds, and once more the mangalsutra that had outlived its purpose, turned into Superman and saved the day. After I returned the money to the bank and got the gold back, I decided to say goodbye to this piece. It had played so many parts in my life, I felt that if I held on to it any longer, it would be with me forever. I didn't relish the thought of a traditional symbol of marriage bailing me out of sticky situations when I was valiantly trying to be single.

I sold it without regret and with an ease that left me quite dumbfounded. In twenty minutes, I had a significant amount of hard cash on me. With that money, I very impractically went on a holiday. There, I watched the sea a lot and let the waves wash out a lot of the debris in me.

When he had tied the mangalsutra around my neck, we had cracked a joke about the whole 'dramatization' of this chain in Hindi movies. The Ex even said a few doormat dialogues. At that point we were happy, confident and not just in love with each other, but also in love with a future we were sure to have.

Today, there is nothing but sadness when I think of that day. I am sure, though, that like the mangalsutra, one day all the emotional muck that the Ex has left in me will disappear. I will wake up to the date of my wedding anniversary and think 'What an ordinary day' and it will be lovely.

The Wedding Album That Was More Resilient Than the Wedding

Seven hundred and fifty bright, shiny rectangular photographs, mounted on hard glossy cardboard, bound in expensive, ugly velvet stood testimony to the happiness a couple had shared one unforgettable day. Neither the happiness nor the couple would survive.

Wedding albums are expensive must-haves of a wedding. It's fine if things go well and the mother can dandle her grandkid on the knee and say, 'Look at your amma and achan before you were born'. Then it becomes worth the trouble.

If you're like me and the marriage ended, luckily before that dandling grandkid came, you're stuck with a 7 kg error that can be used as a small stool.

After the divorce, when I was going through the wedding album (occasionally, as we've seen, I'm a bit of a masochist) I remembered how I had fought with the Kerala photographer who was given the important task of capturing the event for posterity. He wanted me to do the cheesiest things. For instance, one of his demands was that I look out into the distance like a lovesick puppy. He explained that he would take this pose and Photoshop the Ex's picture in front of my eyes so that a 'Waiting for the lover' effect was created. When I refused to do this, he wanted me to sit under a coconut tree, drawing hearts in the mud. Naturally, I didn't oblige. With tears in his eyes he told my mum that I was the most difficult bride to shoot. I felt secretly pleased and every time I looked at him during the wedding and saw his tortured anguish, I'd break into the most beatific bridal smile.

In the album, there is this picture of me wagging a finger at the Ex. It looks incongruous for it is not a normal wedding posture. It seems a bit angry and accusatory. I'm sure the photographer put that picture in to get back at me. I didn't mind for we knew that the gesture was in jest. I was warning him not to cheat at 'Word-building'. We had begun playing this game in the middle of the wedding as we were thoroughly bored with the rituals that seemed to go on for hours and hours. I think at the moment that this photo was captured, the Ex was trying to spell aardvark with a single 'a'.

In that album, there are 250 pictures of us touching various people's feet, mostly relatives, well-wishers and old friends. I can't help thinking what happened to all those heartfelt blessings. Weren't they enough to protect us? Why didn't the goodwill showered on us form a shield and shelter us from the disastrous future we were going to have?

My friends stand in a group snap grinning ear-to-ear. Their tomboy, 'I-will-never-marry' best friend was finally tying the knot. I could see the mirth in their eyes, the gentle teasing smiles.

As my eyes scan their faces, I remember each one's reaction when I told them about the split.

As I flip the pages, the photo of the pujari, looking like a hairy orang-utan, makes me smile in spite of the tears that are flowing silently. He was the oddest creature. He had a battery operated fan, which would blow the puja smoke into our faces, and he would chant his mantras into a handheld loudspeaker, amplifying the already strange-sounding slokas. Every time he'd pause between the chants, we'd celebrate the silence with relief. I contemplated taking a microphone and going to inform him personally, and as loudly, 'The marriage is off! We are dissolved now!'

In my family, we have a tradition of gifting the ladies who are close to us a saree around the time of the wedding. Most people wear that saree on the wedding day. The photos flashed what my loved ones wore and I remembered how I had chosen the sarees. I wondered about when they saw the saree in their cupboard, did they think of it as 'Her wedding saree gift' or 'That divorced girl's saree'. How did the memories rearrange in their head to accommodate this new status?

The photographer has added a picture of me glaring at the Ex with a lot of anger. He is looking equally mad. We were fighting because neither of us had remembered to bring ID cards to register the wedding and were blaming each other. (My mum turned into the Dark Knight and saved the day by having copies of our passports in her purse.) Was the picture a portent of things to come?

The last line in the album is a sentimental phrase, written in cursive writing with garish pink hearts strewn around it. It says,

'True love is endless' and a photograph of us holding hands is juxtaposed on a sandy beach. That's when it hits me. Our love wasn't true or true enough. Is that possible? For things to be temporarily true?

After the tears subsided, I knew I had to destroy this physical evidence of perhaps the biggest mistake of my life. For three hours, with a pair of scissors, I sat and cut the pictures into the tiniest pieces possible.

The next day, the album didn't exist but the memories of the wedding would stay with me only to surface at the unlikeliest of moments. A pink candy, the exact colour of the wedding saree, at a children's birthday party. A certain silk kurta the Ex wore would dance before my eyes on my morning walk. A particular smell, like burnt wood in a short-cut alley, flashed the sacred fire that refused to die out that day.

Unlike the album, I couldn't cut and throw away the memories for they were cut into me, like the branding marks on cattle skin.

Who Gets to Keep Marquis de Sade?

The only wealth we had were books. This may seem beautiful in an idealistic sense but in a practical way it meant paying the movers and packers a king's ransom, an arm and two legs.

We had over two thousand books between us and every book had a place, a time, a reason and a story of how it began to live with us. Before I met the Ex, I was not just a compulsive buyer of books but a compulsive lender too.

The minute I read something fabulous, I would furiously look for a borrower who would love the book as much as me. The Ex taught me to be a scrooge. People were encouraged not to borrow. The few thick-skinned ones who persisted were given our treasures grudgingly. The Ex would then write their names on a post-it, pin it up on the French window and after three weeks would call them, reminding them to return the goods. We rarely lost a book, except for this one time, when a childhood friend of mine borrowed a large stack of books and lost them in transit, along with her gold jewellery. Of course, asking her to replace the books at this point was inconsiderate and luckily, I think to this day, the Ex has no clue about it.

The result was that after thirty years of buying books and not owning a single one, in my thirty-fifth year I had four shelves packed with worlds we could escape into, on demand, at the slightest whim. Dividing this mountain of treasure was a nightmare to say the least. However, unlike the linen, I knew that some of the books were definitely coming with me. There was no way I could leave them behind, especially since I knew that I needed their friendship to survive in these trying times.

When I asked him how we should divide our colossal fortune, he, playing the magnanimous irritant, said that I could take all of them for he had stopped reading. Not to be outdone by his generosity, I decided I'd take the books I loved and leave behind the books he cared for. Only a few would overlap and decisions for them would be made on an individual basis.

It was true though what he said about turning into a non-reader. For after he had brought the Big Problem home, he was too mind-twisted to spend time on any activity he loved. But one day, the reader in him would awaken and at that point I didn't want him to look at empty shelves with regret. I couldn't do something so mean to a reader, it didn't matter if the reader came in the form of an Ex.

A basic division was easy for our book tastes strongly diverged. I like dysfunctional urban stories, women authors, pulp and South Asian debutantes. He likes history, coming-of-age revelations and spy tales. For some inexplicable reason, we both love Jewish writers. I packed four cartons of my books, shocked that I had accumulated this much. For someone who owned a mere four books for the first thirty years of her life (these were the only ones I wouldn't lend and came with me on all my travels), this was a corpus unimaginable. In fact, in the five years with the Ex, this was the only thing I had achieved.

The shelves looked bare after I had taken my share. Unable to bear the hollow spaces, I took out the books from the four shelves and rearranged them in two. The other two shelves were luckily closed cupboards whose doors could be shut. I knew when the Ex would open them he would feel a strong pang of pain, but I couldn't do more. Splitting the stack had been exhausting and he had conveniently wormed out of it. I had to stop empathizing, thinking about him and protecting him. But all of this came so instinctively that it was hard to stop.

I moved on to what I called 'The Mutual Love Pile'. This would be hard to divide, full of moral conundrums and battles with greed. The first set of books, which we both loved, were Sempé. A brilliant cartoonist, we had spent hours reading the books together and chuckling away afternoons. They were expensive books and bought when we had no money. Coveted, saved for and finally owned. I couldn't take all of them and therefore split them in the middle. Two for him, two for me.

Not all the books in the pile were bought in even numbers. To assuage my conscience, for every extra book I took from the pile, I gave him one. Finally, there was one book left – *The Good Soldier Švejk*. In a gust of impulsive generosity, I let him have it. After all, he was the one who spotted it first at that sale.

There were some books that were his but I felt I had a moral right over them. I had read them more than once and adored them much more than he ever did. Though he was the rightful owner, I'd like to think I was their spiritual seeker. Updike's Rabbit series and the Gormenghast trilogy falls under this category.

Andre Gide was an author I hadn't even heard of till I met the Ex. His diaries sustained me through many nights of doubt and lost creativity. These books were part of the Ex's youth but they were my present. With this reasoning, I packed Gide's diaries, with only the slightest twinge of guilt.

We both immensely enjoyed Paul Auster but the Ex was the bigger fan. I knew when he started reading again, these would be the first books he'd reach for. With a heavy heart, I left them behind. To date, I've never bought them again.

The only two books that I stole were Peter Suskind's *Pigeon* and Joseph Roth's *Hotel Savoy*. The Ex liked these books as much as I did. To make it worse one of them was a gift from someone special. I didn't reason on these books. I knew I was stealing them, unfairly, but I persisted. Pure, unforgivable greed.

For those of you who are curious about such things I kept the Marquis de Sade. The Ex said that he didn't need a book to learn how to be sadistic.

As the sun set, that awful day drew to a close and the deed was done. The boxes got packed and taken to my new house. Unpacking a 1000 memories was lovely. I thought it would be painful but books have their own life. As I placed them in their new bookshelves, I forgot about why they had come there. I remembered a lot of stories, phrases and delightful thoughts that they had gifted me over time. They made me feel like I'd walked into my own house, which was waiting for me forever. They were old friends, these books of mine and they were by my side. I didn't think too much about the other 1000 I had left behind. In fact, I didn't think about them at all.

Guess this is what couples who divide real property go through. Whimsically selfish and capriciously illogical, we become little children who want it all.

Are His Mother's Vessels Your Vessels and Other Philosophical Questions

I like black pots. Those non-sticky chrome kinds, sleek and stunningly beautiful. When the Ex's mother heard me oooing and aahing about these kitchen beauties, poor thing, unaware of my non-existent cooking skills, went out and bought a whole range of them.

Over time, I grew to love the black saucepan, which bubbled my tea perfectly, the lovely skillet, which in spite of numerous burnings refused to tarnish or lose its gleam. Omelettes tasted better off it. They were also more obedient, faithfully flopping without breaking. Then, there was the large black monster bowl, almost big enough to sit in, in which I had made biryani for the first and last time. Every time I saw its bulging size, my eyes would glitter fondly at the memory of my successful venture into making the king of food.

When I left the Ex's house, I began missing the black pots and pans. I craved them. Making tea in a steel saucepan didn't feel that good anymore. I went and checked out a few pots in the market but they didn't seem like the ones I had left behind.

The weight wasn't right. The handle felt weird in my palms. It didn't have a single, individual streak that I could love. In those initial days, I missed those pots, especially the saucepan every morning. If it was a bad day, the saucepan would become a metaphor for everything that had gone wrong and a bout of crying was inevitable.

One day, without me asking for it, the Ex came home and dropped off the black saucepan saying, 'I don't drink tea'. He had remembered how much I loved it. As for the skillet and that big black pot, well, I bought my own. I didn't mind much after the saucepan had come home.

There were other gifts that our split had made necessary to deal with. The tasteless sarees, prehistoric kitchen equipment, three Bhagvad Gitas, clocks, tea sets, weird artefacts gifted by numerous aunts and uncles at the time of the wedding. There were many of these in the attic and we had forgotten about them like a bad dream. I sold the whole lot to the *raddiwalla*, the local scrap dealer.

A few gifts, which I found only at the time of the split, were a pleasant surprise. Like the silver anklets that his cousin had given me, buried in a suitcase. Considering how much the price of silver had shot up maybe I should have returned them. The question was to whom should I give them back? To the Ex? That lovely cousin? I did neither. Instead, I wore them and danced in the rain.

An uncle of mine had given the Ex an old Sanskrit-English dictionary printed during the British Raj for the Ex had told him that he loved words. They had met only once and hit it off well, spending the afternoon together, ignoring the other relatives in the room.

This uncle was famous for being extremely eccentric, taciturn and normally avoided everybody. The Ex having made an impact on the old tyrant was much talked about during the initial days of our wedding. Maybe that's why the Ex got that priceless old dictionary. The quandary at the time of the split was whether this dictionary was a family heirloom which had to be returned to the uncle or did the Ex earn it for he had gotten it solely because he had managed to connect with a person the rest of the family found difficult. I chose the latter and now the Sanskrit to English antique guide is the Ex's legacy to give to whosoever he pleases. I have no idea what the uncle thought about the whole thing. When I met him, much later, he continued to be his normal grumpy self and grunted in my direction, not mentioning either the Ex or the dictionary.

A family friend had hit on an innovative wedding gift. A money bond that would mature in ten years. Yes, it was a good investment and it lasted longer than the marriage. I wondered where the Ex and I would be when the bond matured. It's in both our names and we'll have to come together to sign it and get the money.

Most of our gifts had a place, either in his house or mine. The only one that didn't was a musical instrument from Australia. It was the cylindrical branch of a tree, which had a variety of scales and tones along its length. What made it attractive was its polished wooden body, on which was tied at either end large bright coloured strings that shouted 'Not from here'. Gorgeous to look and incredible to play with, it was a conversation starter that we both loved and treasured; envied by every musician who came home, it had pride of place in our hall.

On it were written these corny words, almost like a joke – 'May you make music together, forever, in this life and others'. We had cracked up on the cheesy and slightly nonsensical wording. The friend who had given it to us had gone to considerable pain to carve the entire message neatly without marring the beauty of the instrument.

Neither of us felt like taking it. I didn't want to for I couldn't play the damn thing. The Ex refused to keep it with him for he said that the words choked him up. I was thinking of sending it back when we found the perfect home for it at our favourite pub.

We had met up to have a drink and iron out a few logistical issues when a group at the neighbouring table, who looked like travelling hippies, began entertaining everyone with their music. They had unique musical instruments and as the beer flowed they looked supremely unselfish, hippie-happy and sunburnt.

One of them was particularly gifted. He had a toothy, nutty smile and his voice and playing ability was outstanding. A childlike gaze of innocence that geniuses and ganja addicts have emanated from him. The Ex and I looked at each other and had the same thought.

The Ex jogged home and brought back the instrument. At the end of the night, we paid our bill and presented the surprised musician with the play pole. To say he was thrilled is an understatement. He even knew what it was called, a didgeridoo. When he read aloud the words carved on it, in his accent from a land we had never been to, it didn't sound corny but right. In our honour, he played us a lovely tune on it. That was the last time we heard it.

The most painful gifts to deal with were the ones the Ex had given me when we were in love. Certain books, jewellery, a trinket, a frog couple. I couldn't bring myself to throw away any. I still have them, dotted around my house, waiting to spring memories on unsuspecting days.

One of the frogs had a yellow stomach for I had once spilt curry on it. Even after a good wash, the turmeric in the gravy stuck to its terracotta belly staining it forever. In a sense that was part of its charm – an earth coloured frog with a yellow stomach sitting next to its uncoloured partner.

Both of them had stretched out poses like they were lounging in the sun and sported goofy smiles. Two days before I moved out, the frog with the stain broke. The Ex and I cleared away the pieces together, leaving behind not a trace of its existence. When I left the house, the single frog came with me and now it sits in a corner, holding a small piece of my heart.

VII

HOW I FED ANGER AND OTHER HUNGRY MONSTERS

Shunning the Shrink and Other Bad Moves

With apologies to Charles Dickens, the period of the divorce was the worst of times. All the negative emotions in the universe that were floating around looking for a place to rest said 'hurrah' and came rushing to reside in me with the happy abandon of a thing that has finally found home. Rage, depression, jealousy (towards other people who seemed happy), helplessness, numbness, unhappiness, frigidity, switch-off-edness, disassociation, shut-down-ness, self-pity and many other disgustingly unhealthy feelings became my constant companions and bed mates. Uninvited, these monsters settled down, shrouding me in a fog of such thick malcontent, that I could hardly see myself. The people who loved me and surrounded me with the anxiousness of care were not even registered on the vision scale.

There is no relief from this sorrow. It seems to stretch for an eternity. There is no end in sight and it is impossible to imagine a day when the pain might stop. It became an unshakable companion that accompanied me everywhere.

During this time, a cousin called from the across the oceans. First, she mumbled that she had heard about the 'D'. Next, she went on a long ramble about how these things happened. A friend of hers was in a bitter custody battle, at least there were no kids here and that was lucky. The long and short of that talk was – that I should go see a shrink, there was nothing 'wrong' in it for these were 'modern' times. To make me feel a little better, she also spoke about how she had had a few sessions with these head mechanics when there was stress at work and how that had helped her cope beautifully.

I listened, yes-yessed and hung up cheerfully. I knew she had been set up by the extended family. I, however, also knew my stance on this one. In the worst of my times, when I had hit a depth that I didn't think I'd reach in this life, I had decided that I would not go to a shrink. Especially because a part of my mind was begging for pills to numb the pain inside. The little survivor chip in my head told me that the first step to tackling this four-headed rabid force was to acknowledge that the divorce wasn't such a big problem.

I knew I was depressed at this point. In every depression quiz I had taken, I had scored full marks. Or almost. The only question, which I couldn't tick were the ones on suicide. No matter how bad it got, the biggest 'hope' factor for me was that I was alive, and if there was life, things would always change. They'd have to.

I was petrified that if I did go to a shrink he would put me on antidepressants and considering my addictive nature, any sort of lifeline had to be avoided. I believed that I had the innate ability, the survivalist tendency to get over this wretched shamble, by myself, by my will.

To add to the isolation, I stopped following the wisdom of other people. There was so much advice being sent my way that it was easier to listen to myself. That is one of the biggest lessons the divorce has taught me – to be carefully tuned in to what I wanted and had to say.

I remembered during the days when we lived together, I was desperately trying to find a solution and would have tried anything, right from hypnotherapy to reading tea leaves. I came across a marriage counsellor at work and suggested to the Ex that we go meet one of these professionals. They were trained to make us work. It seemed like a good idea for we were not having much success doing it ourselves. He declined. He said that he didn't want other people poking around in private bits of him. In retrospect, I understand that he didn't want to go because of the shame, because he knew the logical answer, because in a sense, he wanted this marriage to fail.

For me, during this entire period of depression, the only thing that kept me hinged together was life. Breathe in. Breathe out. Nobody can be unhappy forever, unless they like that emotion a lot. I was a sunny child, the one who chased happiness and rainbows. What happened had smudged my rainbow with long, black streaks. It didn't matter for I knew that one day it would change colour. It did but I've saved one black streak for remembrance, for protection.

I recognized that I was stronger than before. My immunity had gotten built up that one year when I had lived with the weight of the Problem. The bottling-up of what the Ex had done, the pickling of sorrow, the silence of a woman desperate to save a marriage had prepared me for the final split more than anything. The worst was already over. Everything that now happened was a bonus, including tears that were shed in a house that was mine. In a house that wasn't shared by the perpetrator of this unhappiness.

Of course, there are consequences to this healing. Whether a shrink would have helped me heal better is debatable but the baggage I carry is one that feels light. Either that or I have hard-won the strength to carry it effortlessly.

These days, any excess negative emotion makes me clam up. I don't deal with it, I shut down internally, a protective closing. This makes me an annoying adversary to fight with for how can you go to war with a person who ignores you?

I have compassion but very little empathy or sympathy. I spent it all on me. I needed it at that time. There are only that many self-hugs allocated to you in one lifetime and I've run out of my quota. If another great, big emotional calamity comes knocking at my door, I'll deal with it with the numbness of survivors.

This process has defined who I am today and no matter what I do, I can't go back to who I was when I first fell in love with the Ex. It's a wretched thing to have been made by depression.

I was watching this animation film. A bullet shot through the creature and left an actual round, physical hole in its body. That's when it struck me that the divorce had left a bullet hole in me, an invisible one. A round hole, where nothing was kept and bits of leftover debris would keep falling out. I don't panic. I have enough of me to carry me through this life.

The trick, I realized, is to be like that cartoon, who pinned a hanky over the hole. Then, with perfect comic timing, it would stick its finger through the hole in its body for a practical reason, like finding a shorter route to scratch its back. The animae had figured out how to live – by becoming one with the hole. To treat it like skin. Soon, I got used to it. Today, I can't imagine me without this gap.

The Meanest Thing I Did Wasn't That Bad

When someone hurts you, there is a deep-seated need to hurt back. If you grow up as a 'well brought-up middle-class Malayali girl', your initial training in those impressionable, young years won't let you commit violence or anything that can land you in jail. Murder, maiming, planting a python in the Ex's cupboard, lacing his Gatorade with arsenic, booby-trapping his badminton racket to self-detonate on court, hiring assassins or resorting to equipment from the torture chambers of the sixteenth century are unfortunately not feasible realities. On the other hand, being magnanimous and trying to secure a spot amongst the saints by turning the other cheek sadly neither satisfies the soul nor the ego.

When I began hurting the Ex initially, I didn't do it deliberately. The breakdown of love just wouldn't let me see the Ex in a kind light anymore. Anything he said or did was a potential springboard for an attack. Once the drug of verbal abuse invaded my system it was difficult to expunge it. He would say something. It would be enough for me to use my inherited gift of sarcasm to retort, to whip back, to create a minuscule, bleeding nick. In my family, our tongues are swords that have won many battles.

This hurting developed into a predictable cycle. Hurt, apologize for the hurt, hurt again. What broke the camel's back and stopped me from using words as weapons was a taxi ride that lasted an hour and a half. The entire ride was a loud slinging match of abuses, accusations, counter-accusations, filthy rhetoric and meaningless insult, hurled both ways at the top of our voices. The world watched, grateful for the drama during the boring traffic jams.

When we reached home, paid the taxi and stumbled out fatigued by our excess of emotion, we had that 'moment'. Instantly, like a flash of illumination, we both looked at each other and saw what we had reduced ourselves to. After that day, neither of us yelled at the other but my need to hurt him stopped only a long time after that. I didn't exercise my vocal chords at him anymore but I did other things.

I truly feel ashamed of this but when the Ex and I would meet to talk about a few 'reality' details we had to iron out, I'd tell him about other people's reactions to the news of the split. Especially, the ones who told me that they 'never liked him' in the first place. In leveraging their pettiness to hurt him, I made myself baser than them.

I wrote long emails to people we knew telling them intimate facts about the marriage that had no business being aired in public. Much later, burdened by guilt I confessed to a best friend about how I had betrayed the Ex's confidences, told to me at the time when the marriage was going good. I knew he would never tell anyone my secrets. Most generously, she said that I was not like those embittered, revenge-seeking ex-wives, who would do something to humiliate their partner; it was what had happened that had made me like this. The bitter truth is that it is 'what has happened' that makes most people 'like this'. I have no excuses, neither do I carry any shame. It's one of those things I've shrugged off, looked ahead and walked on.

In that corner of my head, which needs words like 'blame' to feel peaceful, I hold him responsible. The unfortunate part is, so does he. I have the power to alleviate his guilt and make him feel a bit better, yet I do not do a single thing to ease his pain.

In this list of confessions, one of the pettiest things I did involves clothes. He had two favourite, super expensive sports shirts with technology that made our TV look antiquated. It did various impressive things. Evaporated the sweat, deodorised the sweat smell, got a glass of fresh watermelon juice after the run, etc. I took the scissors and deliberately cut two unnoticeable holes in them. I am ashamed to say that the Ex still wears them unaware of the damage inflicted on their high-tech bodies.

When people talk to me about my divorce, even today, I subtly imply that it was the Ex's fault (I'm sure even this book spells that out, between the lines). I am aware of how covertly I communicate the message but I can't seem to let go of the need. A divorce is never one person's fault. There are too many factors, permutations, combinations, strangulations, which lead to the breakdown and to blame a single individual for one particular incident is incorrect and ungenerous. Yet, I continue to play the blame game.

The one that continues to haunt me is a mocking of his dream that I had played out one very angry afternoon. He had told me about it after a few years of courtship. Fragile, cherished and never shared with anybody in the world it was what he believed in unquestioningly, his beacon of hope that dangled like a pacifier in the future, whose coming true would redeem everything that happened in this difficult world.

Deliberately, callously, that noon, I shred apart his vision. With well-articulated realistic arguments, I dismembered the one thing he held most dear. As he buckled with pain, I continued mercilessly. I stopped after a long time. I remember afterwards he went and slept on his bed, one arm covering his eyes as the tears slowly rolled onto the pillow. I have never felt that wicked in my life.

A year later, I brought up his dream tentatively, fearfully asking him what happened to it. With freshly sprung anguish in his eyes, he told me, 'You were right, it wasn't a practical idea.' I still carry the hope that one day he will forget my words and chase that thing he wanted most.

I know I didn't behave that badly compared to some of the stories I've heard. It consoles me partially but when I look at myself in the mirror, I am painfully aware that I didn't always behave the way my parents had brought me up. I didn't, at every step, follow my code of ethics for perhaps the first time in my life. It is, of course, easy to sweep everything under the carpet of 'It's only human', but we who have trespassed know our sins better than anybody else.

The Saddest FAQs with No Answers

One of the most persistent words that echoes over and over in your head during the 'D' odyssey is the word 'why'. It comes alone or in conjunction with other words – 'Why-Me, Why-This, Why-Him, Why-Now, Why-Can't, Why-Did, Why-Why'.

Some of these questions were stupid enough to have obvious answers, some didn't come with any explanations (even the Ex hadn't a clue about how to rationalize them) and some more philosophical in nature questioned the very fabric of this way of living that society had imposed on me and other human beings, since the beginning of civilization. If you can answer these questions, send me a note.

Why does love disappear? Where does it go? Is there a 'Lost and Found' for love?

Why are your parents the only people who love you forever, the only love you can take for granted? Is that why we have kids so that no matter what our partners do, a part of their love will forever live through their kids and be with us?

How do you learn to love if you don't learn it from your parents?

Why did amma and achan teach me to only save money? And not love?

How does one forget their marriage vows? Is it amnesia? Is it a deliberate ignoring of what you staked your life on?

What do the words 'It just happened' mean? Is it possible for things to 'happen' without your consent?

Why does the intensity of love reduce to almost nothing? How does it evaporate, get hidden, lost or destroyed?

Is all love ultimately a memory?

Why is it that I have still to meet a couple that I think is perfect? Nobody seems completely happy together. With things like jobs, homes, holidays, best friends I can easily find standards that are enviable. I can think of someone who has the job I want or the sense of style I crave or the lifestyle I wish I had or the dream house that would make my happiness complete. To date, I have never seen a couple and thought in my head, 'I want to be like them'.

Why does love make me insane, temporarily suspend my reason?

Is love the most helpless choice I make as a victim of a powerful fate?

Is there nothing I can do to safeguard this love?

Why are there so many articles on 'Keeping a man/woman', 'Making the chemistry last', etc.?

Does real love need this much work?

Why would you want to keep a thing that wouldn't want to be kept?

Why should you fight for anyone's love? Shouldn't they give it naturally, with open fists and an overflowing heart?

Is monogamy fundamentally flawed or are we as humans cursed to fail at it throughout our lives?

Why do people spend their lives being the meanest to people who love them, who live with them?

When does marriage become a social tool, like a life insurance policy, essential but boring?

How can you treat a stranger nicer than your own?

Why do I feel the need to have a lover, when it was this 'love' that caused me the biggest hurt I ever faced?

A comedian once remarked, 'Instead of getting married, I'll find a woman I don't like and give her a house'. There are way too many jokes on marriage/wives/husbands and more often than not, the clichés turn true. In spite of this, most of us go into this institution happily, joyfully and with the greatest hope. Are we not listening to the BIG message here?

Why aren't we taught to live another kind of life when we are growing up? Why don't parents encourage live-ins or child-free lives (especially when they themselves are not models of exemplary coupledom or parenthood)?

A friend of mine once said that ninety per cent of the songs and movies we listen to and see are based on love. Then very flippantly and scarily she added, 'We like to talk most about the things we don't have.'

Is the need to be loved the biggest trick we play on ourselves?

Why are single people pitied in our society and not celebrated for their fantastic courage to depend only on themselves? There is such liberating joy in singlehood, yet we look down upon it and label it selfish, perverted, delusional and abnormal.

Isn't there a cleaner way to love without the drama and pain?

Why are we miserly with our love, hoard compliments from others, afraid of mush, when we have already made the biggest commitment and taken this person worthy of our adulation into our lives?

How many times will I have to love to get it right?

Why do I need a man to come home to? What am I endlessly seeking and for whom?

What guarantee do I have that the next time I love it will stay?

Do people stay together because it's easier than staying apart? Is marriage a convenience like sliced bread that we dress up with words like love, soulmate, happiness, etc.? Is that why it fails for conveniences are replaceable?

I am a different woman at different stages in my life. How can the love stay the same when the person that fell in love and the person she fell in love with have changed? Does love morph according to the changes, adapting and loving each new behaviour? When the human being keeps changing, how can love be permanent?

Why do I know that no matter how many times I ask these questions, when the 'right' person comes along I will fall madly in love and with the same heady passion, plunge again into the biggest commitment I can make?

No matter how many questions I ask, my heart is an optimist and is waiting. All our hearts are. Every bit of history, pain and suffering will be forgotten like a puff of smoke in air for we are silly, sick creatures with permanent amnesia, zero sense and bucketfuls of passion. And we'll gift it all to another human being, trustingly, willingly and blindly to play with again and again.

Breaking the Habits of Love

Human beings are programmed caregivers. Once they establish the pattern of care, it goes into loop and is repeated mindlessly through a lifetime of togetherness. My father, even today when I call him, enquires whether I'm taking my vitamin tablets and always ends the call with a reminder to drink only boiled water. Maybe this comes from having spent his growing years seeing a lot of people die from malnutrition and waterborne diseases.

My mother, on the other hand, will ask me the most absurd questions. She'll enquire whether I've had a bath. Irrespective of me telling her a million times that I am old enough to run a house and make decisions that will affect the future of other employees, she continues to demand to know whether my T-shirt is ironed.

There is a couple who live next door to me. The woman is an over-anxious sort and when going out of station, she repeats a hundred little pointless nuggets: 'The chicken is in the freezer, don't order from outside, your stomach will go bad', 'Wash the dog on Sunday', 'Ask the maid to change the bed sheet', 'Don't pay the air conditioner mechanic till he fixes the grunting sound'. The person listening to this, usually grunts, just like the air conditioner.

Doesn't anybody ever stop to think that this advice is being given to a fully grown, functional adult? Someone who is trusted with the greatest authority in their office, who is depended upon for the running of the business. However, we like to put them in a corner of 'helplessness', where without our 'loving' reminders they would fall apart.

This is the biggest lie we tell ourselves. Most people are survivalists, sufficiently capable of taking care of themselves. For example, take the 'chicken in the fridge' advice. If he gets tired of eating out then he'll take that beloved chicken out of the freezer, thaw and eat it. Or he may cook a dish that he read off the net at home. If he can't cook, he'll continue eating out and when the lady who prepared this wonderful chicken returns, he will appreciate her even more than before. Well, if not her, then her cooking.

I think people are scared that if they leave their loved ones to themselves without doling out pointless advice their individual worth will diminish. I'm not asking people to be uncaring, but simply to be sensible about this overflow of concern.

I think most people don't get that it's not such a big deal if he doesn't change the sheets or pick the towel off the floor or doesn't keep the eggs in the fridge in the egg rack. My formula is simple – if I don't like the way something is done, I'll do it myself, instead of nagging an individual who has a different way of operating to do it my way. This isn't being autocratic. I'm sure no couple, no individual on the planet wants to spend precious moments of life engrossed in a discussion about the correct place for the egg. Yet so many of us do it. Over and over again. Make the unimportant important and fritter away time with the unwanted. Me included.

We inherit our parents' programming of love. Our society teaches us that concern is checking whether the loved one has combed his hair. Not peering into the cranium under that tidied hair and seeing if there are any worry weeds that we can pull out.

A friend of mine who had a baby complained bitterly to me that his wife only wants to talk about the baby's bowel movements. I understand, it is important to talk about the digestion of your progeny if there is a problem. But if there is not, why not chat about the exciting world we live in, about politics, art, music? At this point, I can imagine my well-settled, happily married friends roll their eyes and say 'real life doesn't work this way'. Why shouldn't it? Who stops us from pursuing a more meaningful life than the one we have? Yes, you got that answer right. Nobody.

Another friend told me that she loves her husband because she can tell him every thought in her head. I felt sorry for the poor guy. The number of inconsequential thoughts that flit through our minds is staggering. Imagine being subjected to each and every one of them! I'd like to know what the poor chap thinks. Does he tell her every thought in his head?

A colleague of mine calls her husband every day to ask him what he ate and 'How was it?'. Their conversations never last more than twenty seconds and, I noticed, he never asks her the same question. It has become a ritual expression of her love to him. Every day, dutifully, she makes that call without realizing that it has lost any semblance of meaning and is now just a habit, like arranging paper clips in a certain way while speaking on the phone.

As a social experiment, I tried this on one of my wonderfully cooperative friends. For the past ten years, every time her husband stepped out she had asked him to take his umbrella. One day I asked her not to say anything. Too surprised to protest, she kept quiet. He, in his typical fashion, left without the black curved cover. She went ballistic, blaming me for the cold he would catch when that rain fell. I asked her to wait. He came back quite happy, unaware of the drama.

The next day I asked her again to say nothing. The guy, oblivious of the experiment, stepped out of the house and immediately, unexpectedly, came back in. He said that the day looked cloudy, so he thought he should take his umbrella. My friend watched dumbfounded, but the fault was hers. She should have trusted a man who had educated his daughter in such a way that she could live an independent life in one of the toughest cities of the world, a man who had planned for their old age so that the only worry she had was whether he had taken an umbrella when he stepped out. She should know that such a far-thinking, sensible husband would be able to take care of himself too, without her ministrations.

These habits of love are hard to break. Of course, a divorce is a very high price to pay for this lesson, but I'm glad that since I was paying the price anyway, I had at least learnt something along the way. The split taught me to re-look at love and how I used to be as a partner. While on the surface I was doing the 'normal' things, I was shocked by how banal married life had made me and the mundanity that I had unintentionally brought into my marriage.

For example, every time the temperature dipped, did I need to remind him to take his homeopathy tablets? If he was falling sick, long and often enough, I'm sure he would have taken them in self-defence. For almost a year after the divorce, I would think about the stupid little advice tips I had filled his life with. Certain dates would trigger, knee-jerk advice-memory flashes, and I'd have to restrain myself from calling and telling him what to do that day.

This is the pointless advice I used to fill our lives with, which would masquerade in the guise of 'I care'. You can see how meaningless it is:

It's the fifteenth of the month, make your dental appointment. (If he cared about his vanity and personal hygiene he would have done it on his own.)

It's the twenty-fourth, call your cousin in Sydney and wish her a happy anniversary. (If she was that important, he would remember.)

Have you locked the door? (Why did I have to check this? He had taken care of a house before I was in his life without getting it burgled.)

There is cholera in the city, don't eat roadside pani puri. (He reads the papers, he's a big boy.)

What's wrong? (The inevitable question that pops up if he stares into the distance for more than five seconds. If things were troubling him he'd tell me and if he didn't want to that should have been okay too.)

Return X's movie, you've kept it for over two months now. (This was a transaction between two friends, I had no business poking my nose into it, but I did.)

Your cheques are hitting this month, make sure you have adequate balance. (If I didn't remind him and the cheque bounced, then he would make sure that the next time the funds would be there.)

Dry your hair properly, it is still wet. (By now he should have learnt how to have a bath.)

Unfortunately, these habits of love are the knots that keep many marriages together. Mine was no different. It was only when I started remembering the advice I used to give him, I realized how unimportant it was.

I had left him, he was fine.

He had left me, I was fine.

We were both living our lives, quite well, without those daily reminders of love.

VIII

THE NEW NORMAL

Moulting

I was a lucky one to whom nothing really bad had happened till I got married. This helped me have the longest childhood of all. I could be unreasonable, impulsive and excitable, free to chase the butterflies I saw glittering in our world well into my adult years. When I got the divorce, along with the court order, I received a part of me that was changed forever. A divorce is as life-changing as getting married, and this is ironic but true. It is as time-consuming as having a child, with none of the joy. It is as humiliating as being asked to the stage for an award and then having that medal snatched away in the same public glare. When I met old school friends afterwards who gushed, 'You haven't changed at all', I would feel the tears welling up at the sharp thought that I had. You can't see it but I have. How else could it be? I had gone through a journey that was as frightening as difficult. At the end of it, I didn't even like glitter that much.

The good part about a long childhood is that I knew what was good for me. I could see things of innocence – giddy joy, wonder, laughter, carefree abandon, play – and be aware of their priceless value in an adult world. That's why, even through the worst days I was convinced that when I came out of this, it would be better.

These were strange and confusing changes, but with each

one of them, I fought for me. For instance, I went through a point in the divorce when I used to view everything through the 'what's the point' lens. If you haven't gone through this, trust me, it's a real killjoy. I had to disgorge my insides to get this biting pessimism out. It fought and raged within me. I used up every trick in the book including, 'It irritates people when you are happy' (which is a fact: I had noticed the moral twerps feeling very, very unhappy when I didn't). My sick mind latched on to that and started chasing fun, pretend-finding rainbows.

Excitement is underrated. When I began pushing my buttons to take holidays, to try out a new bakery, go to a snake park and touch those cold, calm creatures, I began to walk once again with the abandon of a girl racing the wind. To me, it felt important to be passionate about life and what it has to give.

If only to convince myself that I was alive, I took up French class. My enrolment upped the class average by five years. Five times a week, I sat on a bench with sixteen-year-olds who were over-doused in hormones and blatantly contained sexual attractions. Looking at them, it was interesting to spot the diva, the follower, the loner, the-quietly-sure-of-herself-girl-who-was-already-an-individual, the one-who-everybody-had-a-crush-on-except-himself, a microcosm of our world. Our lives are but patterns and stereotypes repeated many times over. For two hours, people-watching and pure knowledge filled my head. I would go home, do homework and learn my verbs.

Depression is a meanie. When it had me, it forced me to do nothing so that its power could increase in daily doses. Beating it was about doing things, about distracting my mind from the pain, about understanding that this world I lived in didn't operate according to my mood swings. If I wanted to be miserable and sulk in the corner, I could. If I shed the quicksand of blackness and walked into the carnival, the world was there, waiting to accept me with its free rides and other surprises.

There were many things in shambles in me but I tried to repair whatever I could. Thoughts such as 'Men are bastards', 'How do I trust again', 'I don't believe in love', 'There is no such thing as forever', 'Am I attractive?', 'Is it my fault?', 'Can I never keep a relationship?' were thrown out. Deliberately, one by one. These and a million other thoughts are designed to make you feel like one of the dead. Think about it, which sentence is healthier: 'I can never trust again' vs 'I've survived the worst, what am I afraid of now?' Not just healthier, it is also truer.

The other fact that spurred me on was that five years of my life were gone, wasted. I couldn't get them back. The five years hadn't been all unhappy but the truth that stared me in the face was that if the marriage hadn't happened, I would have been better off. Much better off. Learning to live well was like a sweet revenge.

This emotional moulting shed the unhappiness and gave me fresh skin. Parts of it were designed like the old me, but there were other bits, which were new, which were precious, for they had come at the cost of my life. Keeping my temper, holding the people I loved close, treating my loved ones the best, never taking love for granted, finding little pockets of happiness in each day were landmark lessons.

The divorce taught me to be kind, gently kind, achingly kind, for we are all fragile creatures, easily crushable, each one of us with our thumping, large hearts, yearning with imperfection, craving for so little and being terribly bruised all the time.

Divorce Isn't Contagious

It was a million times removed cousin's wedding and my mother was pressurizing me to go. After the divorce, I had become allergic to the seemingly ceaseless family functions. I avoided birthdays, pujas, receptions and marriages with a single-minded dedication. One reason was that these were events where people, moral twerps among them, gathered to talk about marriage, birth and death.

I should have heeded the good counsel I had given myself but my mother, persistent and optimistic, played her trump card. She said that a cousin's great grandma, who was not going to live to see another grandkid's wedding, had specifically asked for me.

The honour of the invitation was obvious. She was a revered spirit, respected by the entire family. When I was younger, she had consistently been one of my big supporters, encouraging me to study, do what I want, marry late. I knew that even if I had chopped off a few heads, she would have cheerfully called me home to have her amazing, rich red fish-head curry. The grand matriarch had spoken, and I was still a favourite.

I donned the customary silk saree and matching gold bands on the ears and neck. Glaring down my mother's attempts to put an extra gold chain around my neck, I marched into the den of kanjeevaram sarees and crisp, cream veshtis.

In our custom, the bride is escorted on to the stage, where she stands beside the groom, by other young women, married and unmarried, holding various symbols that are auspicious. Usually, I was picked to be one of these women. This time, the bride's mother, my aunt, deliberately ignored me and called out to the other girls.

The truth was that I didn't even want to carry that damn lamp and walk puppet-like in front of the bride. But it made me feel bad about myself. Vulnerable, and now hurt, I could feel the tears shining in my eyes. That's when it hit me that the only other 'close' relative who wasn't in the escort committee was a young widow. Unlike me, with my opportunities, she lived in her dead husband's home in the village. She had a resigned look on her face, she didn't care. I felt a bit ashamed. It was the first time I was conscious of her non-inclusion in ceremonies. In fact, it was the first time I was conscious of her. The silent sitter in the corner, who had found an escape in her head to avoid this ugly world they kept dragging her into.

In spite of seeing the widow, my rage continued to escalate. I don't think anybody noticed. Silent insults are felt only by the person receiving them and by the person giving them. Everybody else was busy enjoying the functions to be concerned about these small dramas, the side acts of any social setting.

I would have continued to feel stormy throughout the wedding, if it wasn't for an eighty-seven-year old wrinkled arm that tucked into mine. It was the great grandmother. Chuckling, she told me that she wished she was of a time when she could have divorced her husband and left the village. I had heard stories of how insufferable he was and how she had stood up to him with the courage of a panther. We walked away from the wedding, sat outside enjoying the breeze and talked about life. She spoke, I listened. I forgot I wasn't asked to carry a lamp.

The incident prepared me to not expect everyone to understand. I think of the world I come from as liberal and progressive, completely accepting, and it was a shock to meet a petty, mean person. Today, I am careful about which family functions I go to. Who I reach out to.

It took a while to get used to saying that I was 'divorced'. The word does have a nasty ring to it. It somehow suggests failure, and moral corruption. A friend of mine, who lives in another part of the world, told me that when she got divorced, she had no problem saying it. For her, it was the same as being single. For me, it was not the case. I think it has got to do with how this term is viewed in Indian society.

When you are single it means you haven't met the right person, but being divorced means you made a big mistake. It's as humiliating as a wardrobe malfunction: when you walk you can hear the shocked 'Oooos' following you, reminding you what a moron you have been. It doesn't matter whose fault it is. When my marriage got dissolved, I was to blame. (This isn't a sexist thing. I am sure for the Ex, in his family, he is to blame.)

To combat this reluctance to refer to myself as a divorcee, I tried looking into the mirror and calling myself 'Divorcee' loudly, ten times every morning. Initially, I'd be a bit startled. It would sound harsh, like a bad taste on my tongue. On days when I couldn't bear it, I'd kid around and call myself a fashionable 'Miss D'. Slowly, the exercise worked. The word 'divorcee' began losing its power and I started getting comfortable with the tag. A slight sting however lingered. What ultimately cured me was a friend of mine who explained it this way:

'Being divorced is like being a soldier. It means you have fought for your right to happiness. You have faced depression, a blow to your confidence and ego, and emerged stronger and triumphant. Instead of being a coward and living with injustice, you have raised the bar for your own life, and by doing so, given yourself a chance to move towards a greater happiness. The rest of your life will be better, for you will always know how much worse it could have been.'

I almost felt like applauding at the end of this speech; instead I wrote it down and stuck it up on my mirror. Now when I say divorcee, I always add soldier in my head. A sense of bravery and goodwill floods into me and suddenly, to quote the song, 'I don't feel so bad'.

There were occasions when I used to say that I was single. They were: when I would meet old school teachers, especially the ones whose classes I had aced – I'd hate them thinking that I got an 'F' in marriage; when I would bump into very, very old people who were only acquaintances – they were probably going to die soon, they didn't need to be burdened with real world crap.

The single tag also worked for people who provide services – plumbers, painters, real estate agents, gas connectors, landlords, bankers, insurance agents, travel agents, maids, cooks, etc. Single is what they can digest, without converting it into local gossip and single is what they get.

But all these terms, 'Single', 'Married', 'Divorced', have no value whatsoever. What I have realized is that in this long and complicated life, the only term that makes sense that is worth the journey of a thousand heartaches, is 'Happy'.

The P's and Q's of Getting a D

Mrs Castalino for four years taught our class the P's and Q's of the English language (Please, May I, Thank You, etc.). She quizzed us so much on it that every one of my forty classmates could pass an Emily Post test. I am sure she would have never imagined what a critical role it would play in my life. I think by maintaining a standard of civility, I contained the highly volatile process of getting a divorce. These are a few phrases that came handy and helped to smoothen more than a few bumpy conversations.

Please will you stop being such a twerp and meet me halfway on this.

Thank you for your concern, but what I do after this is entirely my business.

I'm sorry you miss me, but we can't do anything about it now, can we?

I understand your mum is upset, but no, I cannot talk to her. She will be able to understand what her son says better.

Yes, I miss the good old days too, but I am at work and will speak to you on this later.

Please stop being such a horrible, self-absorbed person. It would help me if you got your head out of the gloom cloud and faced reality.

I appreciate what you are saying but you have no idea what I feel about you. 'Hate' is too simple a word. Discussing this with you won't help me, so please don't bring up my feelings again.

It would be great if you didn't ask me how I am. In case you are wondering, remember you have kicked me in the stomach and I am rolling on the ground in pain. Permanently. Thanks for asking.

I'm sorry they blamed you but so do I. Can we now decide about what to do with the didgeridoo we got as a wedding gift? Do you want to keep it?

I do not know how many couples break-up every year. I do not intend to spend my time wondering about which part of the statistic I am. Can you please stop dithering and tell me if you want the didgeridoo?

I'm sorry I won't be able to go to your friend's wedding with you. Yes, it will make him very happy to see us together but it will make me very sad. If you don't mind, I prefer choosing my happiness over his.

I am so angry with you right now I don't want to say another word.

Please do not get philosophical with me. We are dealing with a very real problem here, it's called our life.

I'm sorry I'm not going to engage in name calling. Nobody is responsible for what happened, except us. Dragging in other people and incidents of yesterday will not justify what we are doing to our marriage.

I'd appreciate it if you could come with me when I tell the people who set us up in the first place how wrong they were about us. Yes, I can do it alone but I don't want to.

When my mother rings, please hear her out and do not get angry. She is an old woman and saying what is on her mind will help her feel a little bit better.

I am truly sorry your friend passed away and I am here in case you need me.

I knew instinctively that a tornado of rage would splinter me from the inside. To survive I had to hold on to my manners. It was extremely critical not to lose myself and fire words that would burn, for they would burn me more. So I started walking out of conversations when I was extremely angry. If I thought of something derisive and mean, I wouldn't say it. Instead, I would go to the bathroom and tell the flush. That poor thing, what all it had to hear. Every time I felt like I wanted to throw things at his head, I'd go for a walk. My new mantra was kill the calories, not the Ex.

I began being wary of people who would say too many mean things about the Ex. I didn't want to fire my negativity with more negativity. I stopped thinking of him in my head as 'the bastard'. Having said that, somehow I didn't like thinking of his name either, it felt too intimate, so I settled for 'that guy'.

The end result was that because I wasn't mean, spiteful and vengeful, I began to heal faster. I focused on my pain, not the reason for it. I taught myself the obvious – he wasn't filling my mind with sadness, I was. By making myself the sole custodian of my happiness, by absolving him of his role in the catastrophe my life had turned into, I became responsible for my mood swings. Now that the onus was on me, I worked extra hard to find my happiness bug.

The good manners I scrupulously maintained brought a certain dignity to what is a messy procedure. I must admit, they made me feel hugely superior. I think I overused them for it would annoy the hell out of the Ex. This was extremely petty but it was so gratifying. While he stumbled, a dithering, bumbling mass of emotion, I'd calmly ask if he wanted a cup of tea. Or if he went on a 'What have I done to our life' rant, I'd listen not sharing his extreme despair. This was much later, when I had become desensitized, for I think there is only that much crackle you can listen to about the same topic.

The result of all this civility is that the Ex and I can have a polite conversation. Occasionally, he calls up to enquire about my health and happiness. We have both moved on in what I think is a mature adult way.

My friends and family are amazed by what has transpired. Since we are not bitter, they have learnt not to be. What happened is done, dusted and kept in the shelf of things I don't want to remember. We will carry the scars of this encounter our entire lives, but both of us know that if it weren't for manners, it would have been worse. Much, much worse.

Shushing the Biological Clock

I never wanted children till I lost a husband. After that I couldn't stop being hungry for them, needing them at an almost desperate level. Ever noticed how the minute you start wanting a particular thing, you see it everywhere. My desire multiplied the kids on earth, for suddenly they were all around me. I saw them kicking stones on the footpath, making a ruckus at restaurants, gazing into the sky outside pubs, running about in shopping malls, riding trolleys at the grocery store, juggling onions at the veggie market, gulping down pani puris larger than their faces at the best pani puri-seller, crying their heart out in a bus. Wherever I went, they appeared. It was amazing. With their cute clothes, innocent smiles and heartbreaking haircuts, they made me wish and wish for one of my own.

I wondered whether this sudden need for children was because I wanted a love that would never leave me, a permanent love that wouldn't walk out on me one day. Kids are hostage to your love till they turn twenty-one and after that you can hold them through guilt. My parents had me still. I knew that no matter how indifferent a caregiver I would be, I'd at least, for a tiny bit of time, be the most important thing in their universe.

Was this sudden need to have kids only to feed the empty hollow in my heart? I am not sure. Maybe it was my biological clock, which had been screaming all along, finally being heard. I had ignored it for so long, it was perhaps the silence of my sadness that brought out its voice. It doesn't matter what the reason was. I wanted a child and I had wiped out the existence of a man from my life, who could have given me this very gift. I couldn't help feeling a little bitter.

The Ex and I had never discussed having a child. We were busy, we were living it up. We were partying, working hard and we had zero responsibilities and liabilities. A child meant giving up our lifestyle and we were not ready to do so at that point. In fact, after friends would have children, we'd go out of our way to avoid them. It's not that we weren't fond of kids. We were happy to entertain them as long as they could be returned. Would a child have kept the marriage together? Who knows and now it is too late to contemplate things of that nature.

One of the things I promised myself after the divorce was that I'd never compromise on my happiness again, I'd try to fulfil whatever I desired, I'd work really hard to make my wishes come true. Now here was I with this totally unreasonable need.

I was aware with a sickening thud in my heart that I was at the fag end of my reproductive years. My age mocked me with visions of those times when I had scoffed at being a mother and danced into the wee hours in parties, footloose and unaware of the trampling of time.

It was scary. The divorce had emptied me of positivity and the little bit that remained was being eroded by this single thought. I was getting obsessive and I was again sliding into that dangerous depression I had crawled out of. Before I could tumble through that dark hole, I saw a BBC documentary where a scientist said that he didn't want kids, his genes could go jump in a lake.

This was a small sliver of light. If I could not have my own kids, I could adopt when I was ready. When I was financially secure. This need to have my own kid was what the world had foisted on me, like marriage. I had thrown off one shackle, I could effortlessly throw off the other.

In a frenzy, I began reading about adoption and single women. Before I took it to the next level, reason prevailed and I calmed myself down. I knew that there was no way I could afford a child. Not yet, at least. Also, I wanted to test my intentions. It couldn't be a whim, a desire that would fade away the minute it was satisfied.

If I brought a child home, it would be a commitment I'd have to honour every day for the next twenty years and perhaps all my life. Most people have children without too much thought. They do it for it is the next stage of their relationship or because they forgot to use a condom or they got bored partying or because their friends were procreating and they didn't want to be left out on this latest adventure. Isn't it amazing that the most important job in the world requires no qualification? The insanely difficult task of bringing up a whole new human in the world is the right of anybody who can make love. It is a miracle of creation that the world rests on the shoulders of a lucky ova and sperm.

A few days of intense research and I felt a lot calmer. According to Indian law, I could adopt till I was forty-five.

That was a gazillion years away. I had time, and two-three years down the line, if I wanted a child, I'd go ahead and bring one into my life.

I had to make sure that the child wasn't being brought in to plug the hollows of my heart but that she was being invited home from a genuine need to care and look after her (yes, I'd only adopt a girl child). It wouldn't be fair to impose a needy love on an unsuspecting innocent. I had the luxury of time to clear my head and understand the exact truth behind my desire to adopt. For now, I could be calm and secure in the knowledge that I had an option. That I didn't have to live with regret and I didn't need the Ex or anybody else for this. Phew!

Wearing Undies for Dinner

Loneliness is pathetic and crummy. Aloneness is exciting and exotic. I read in a study that, increasingly, people are choosing to live alone, and why not? When you think of the number of flaws that fill an average human being, it seems a sensible thing to do – live with yourself, where the only dysfunctions you have to deal with are the ones you own.

Two weeks after I moved into my apartment, my cousin called. She enquired about what I was doing. I told her I was eating chips for dinner and reading a book. Enviously, she asked, 'There's nobody at home, right?'

'Nope.' I was feeling perfectly sunny and content.

She sighed. She'd give anything to swap places with me. It's easy, I told her, all she had to do was divorce her husband and give the custody of her kids to him. She half-joked, 'I wish.' After we hung up, I couldn't stop grinning. To the few old aunties in the building who used to look sympathetically at me and ask, 'Don't you miss people? And I heard you have no television too', I would cheerfully hoot, 'No, I like it this way'. And I could see the mental thank yous to the gods on their faces for ensuring that their rude daughters and demanding husbands lived with them.

When I first started living alone, I'd as usual hug the far corner of the bed, leaving the larger expanse for the now missing Ex. One day, in my sleep I sprawled and suddenly discovered that there was no body obstructing my stretch. Luxuriating with the confidence of a cat, I took up as much room as the five foot two inches of me could. This bed was now my kingdom and I wasn't that small mouse on the edge of a four-poster. Living alone tested the limits of my laziness and took them to unimaginable heights. After being a responsible adult for so long, I found that sliding into teenage sloth was restful and easy. Stay in bed all day, order in, leave the empty boxes around the bed, eat chocolate, drool on the pillow, watch the light change in the room and do, yes, nothing. Oink!

When I was with a loved one, it was extremely difficult to do this 'nothing'. The other person in the room usually wants attention. He will have things to share, or we'll cuddle together or clean up. It's a different kind of relaxation. This don't-move-a-muscle-go-comatose-in-bed can only be done alone, for it has to be enjoyed guilt-free. Of course, it's not done every weekend, for we single people are busy with our happening lives filled with concerts, plays, socializing, hobnobbing and making plans at the drop of a hat … but it can!

When you live with yourself the only rules that are to be followed are the ones you make. Friends can drop in anytime without worrying about the partner's mood or need to rest. I used to tell the maid to take the day off if I didn't feel like seeing anybody and wanted to curl up with a book and read. In one marathon reading session, I finished *The Lord of the Rings* in forty-eight continuous, nail-biting, page-turning hours.

Within my four walls, I had the freedom to carry out my darkest, most secret thoughts every day. I must say I was surprised by what a boring person I turned out to be. The wildest thing I did was consume a bottle of wine and fill the house with strips of paper with poetry written on them. The next morning when I woke up, the paper pieces fluttered in the breeze. I took the day off and read my words. A few things were pretty good, some terribly maudlin and others clearly the illegible scrawls of a drunk.

Yes, I did miss the Ex and I did feel lonely, but those negative emotions were losing strength as I began to enjoy me and my space more.

I'd love to go to the old book market, especially on the first Sunday of the month and buy fifteen books. What I had bought wasn't reading material but sheer weekend pleasure. A friend of mine, most concerned, told me that I was avoiding reality and escaping from the world. I didn't care. It was such a delightful getaway and it improved my vocabulary. You can't argue with the veracity of that.

The good part about being a reading addict is that nobody will tell me to stop. It's not bad for health, it doesn't make me put on weight, lose my mind and manners, give me a headache the next day or infuse me with false confidence to do stupid stuff. If my amma calls and asks what I am up to and I tell her that I'm reading, she hangs up confident that her little 'un isn't up to no good. Instead, imagine if I told her I'm finishing a bottle of whisky. She'd catch the next flight and be at my doorstep.

One evening, I was wondering what to do when my eye suddenly caught the calendar and I saw that it was a year since the divorce. I felt a whoosh of relief in me. Gratitude for having escaped those dark, dreary days intact. I looked at my book collection, which had tripled, the flat I loved, the cook who was a whiz, a job that paid the bills and a life that was more happy than sad. I almost wanted to get down on my knees, kiss the floor and thank the gods for this bounty.

I decided not to be so melodramatic but I wanted to celebrate the day. I had a bottle of very good wine, which I was saving for a special moment. I opened it and poured it into the fancy wine glass I had bought. The red sparkled with life and smelt of celebration. I raided the fridge. I found half a bar of imported chocolate, a crumbling brownie, three excellent pieces of cheese and four individual French fries. To add a little style, I slit a few olives and placed one on each fry.

I lit candles in a square and sat in the middle, a goddess in my kingdom of one person. I arranged my meal around me including the bottle so that I wouldn't have to get up for a refill. I switched off the lights in the house and the shadows on the wall played tricks with the candle flame. I watched myself being reflected around this room of freedom, looking like a black siren in ultra-hot underwear. Then, lifting up my wine glass, I toasted to myself and had one of the best dinners of my life.

IX

TRIPPING ON HIGH HEELS

The Short Black Dress Doesn't Even Go Around My Neck

I had been with the Ex for five years and along the way I had lost the need to look good every waking minute. In my twenties, the pursuit of enhancing my attraction was a serious indulgence, right down to matching tee and shorts for the night. I worked at it so much I could almost call it a profession. As time shimmered away into the distance, in a little black dress, dressing up became mostly a 'throw-and-go', which simply means grab the nearest ironed top, slip on a pair of jeans and that's 'ready'. For the night, the Ex's T-shirts were perfect to slumber in and slobber on delicious dreams. As for make-up, I may have occasionally looked into the mirror to check whether spinach was stuck in my teeth, but that was about it. It is amazing how one man's love can take away your vanity and when that love disappears, the vanity pops back, with more force, as if it had never, ever gone anywhere.

After the divorce I got obsessed. Every mirror I passed, I'd stare and note the wrinkles, the drying skin and the appearance of spots, like in those anti-wrinkle ads. Linked to this was a deep-seated insecurity that being older now I wasn't attractive enough to step into the dating game.

I wasn't one of those divorcees who swore off men and hated them with a vengeance. I had made a mistake with the Ex but I felt that there was no reason why I would repeat it. I had enough good male friends to believe that not 'all men are bastards'.

So, while I wasn't scared of dating, I was a bit confused. I didn't know how attractive I was. It was like going back to college but in the mid-thirties. What do I wear? How do I fit in?

Before, I'd see myself through the Ex's lens and he found me attractive enough (though he had stopped saying so. A long time ago. Maybe, it was something I took for granted, maybe it wasn't true, maybe ... maybe ... who cares). After, I had to view myself with what I thought would be the world's gaze, which is basically my own critical eye. The number of photographs I'd take of myself on the phone is not funny. Then, I'd close my eyes, open them and try to look at myself as a stranger would. On some days, I'd think, this is a woman who looks good, a woman I'd like to go out with, an attractive, interesting person. On other days, especially if I would have been crying or feeling low, I'd look into the mirror and see a pathetic creature. I'd compound the sadness: 'I'm the oldest and ugliest person around', 'I look jaded and jaundiced', 'I'd hate to meet me', 'Am I pretty?' A part of me didn't want to curb this obsession. The intense desire to look good was essential to getting over the Ex. He had been the rock I hid under. Exposed to the sun, I wanted to wear the chameleon's orange and yellow, not the grey of the rock. At least, I wanted to be what I thought was 'good-looking'.

The first step to this was that I started paying more attention to my clothes. Relying on my sartorial ingenuity, I bought a pair of purple pants. I wore them to the office and my boss painfully, almost sheepishly, informed me that though he understood I was the 'creative' sort, could I please refrain from purple pants in the corporate office? I obliged and came the next day in red trousers.

When I went back home to my parents', I rummaged through their suitcases, the suitcases themselves the age of antiques. Much to my glee, I found a bunch of clothes from college. I immediately tried them on. A few of them fit (whoopee!), some were too appalling (to what use could I ever have put a brown and red Chinese kimono?), and a handful wouldn't even go around my wrist.

Had I been so thin to carry off this black dress that looked like a hanky? Where had the meat on this bone come from? I wasn't eating an ox a day. Even if I had starved for a whole year, I'm sure I wouldn't have fit into that dress and a lot of other superb clothes that my mother had carefully preserved. I asked my mum whether I actually wore these things. She rolled her eyes in a gesture of long-suffering see-what-I-had-to-put-up-with. Wow! No way are my kids getting to wear anything like that!

Clothes were beginning to affect my mood. When I'd wear a long, trippy, happy skirt I'd feel lovely. I'd swirl around the room, pleased with myself. If I wore those old, fraying brown pyjamas, I would stay in bed, look at the walls and pretend to be a bit of moulding moss. I began paying attention to the clothes that made me feel good. I shed the jeans and began wearing Aladdin pants (harem pants, if you must), hippie tops, styles that were a little flower-power girlish, and told the 'does it suit me' doubt to go hang itself.

As my wardrobe changed, I sensed myself getting better. Even on the days I stayed at home, I dressed up and preened for the walls. Are all divorcees well-dressed? Not necessarily. I know some particularly shabby ones and they don't seem to be adversely affected. These are personal choices and should remain that way.

As for me, my sense of style was redefined because I needed to feel confident, strong, attractive and totally in control of life. I wanted to feel secure, joyful and blessed. I wanted to feel that this life was a gift that I was lucky enough to live. And I wanted to dress in a way that would speak this.

I know it worked, for a friend of mine wryly commented, 'At least the divorce has improved your fashion sense.' Yes! Slam dunk!

The Haircut That Cost an Arm, a Leg and a Head

It is a truth universally acknowledged that if you can't change your life you should change your hairstyle. I do not know where I get my philosophies from but I have absolute belief in them. As the giddy-headed romance of staying alone, doing up the apartment, and living a brand new life began to fade, I needed a distraction. Something that, if it didn't cheer me up, would be a new reason to get depressed. I was so tired of sulking about the Ex.

After thinking about new ways I could torture myself, I settled for the worst one – I decided to get a haircut at a place I had never been to before. If you can't fathom the risk I was taking, you are either one those 'it's-just-dead-cells, it-will-grow-back' enlightened persons, or you've had the same hairstyle since school or you are bald. Me? I was going to let some random person with piercings and pink hair impose their personality on my scalp. I didn't shiver once. I was a divorce-soldier. What's a haircut?

The first thing involved in chopping off the tresses (a grand word for falling thinness that barely managed to cover the scalp) is research. I spoke to friends, Googled, checked out haircuts in magazines, poured through countless photographs looking for that one image that would leap out of the page and scream, 'this is you, this is how you are destined to look'. After an intensive week of seeking, I found four pictures, each of which had a particular feature I wanted – the sides from one photo, the back from the other, etc. I learnt much in the process. I now knew the recommended length for my forehead and for my nose shape. For the first time in my life, I hoped I wouldn't lose any weight because the hair that would frame my face was chosen after a careful measurement of the puffiness of my cheeks. And god forbid, if after this haircut, I forgot to tilt my chin the right way, all would be lost.

The next obstacle was finding the haircutter. I took the normal route for this. I lurked around shopping malls till I found someone who had a haircut I liked and asked her where she cut her hair. It did involve spending small sums on buying more things I didn't need (salespeople look at you suspiciously if you walk into their shop every day and walk out without buying anything). But I prowled intensely, staring strangers in the face and chatting up unsuspecting shoppers.

One woman who had the most awesome hairstyle told me that her mother did it for her, but she lived in another country. While on most days I'm willing to shell out a fortune for my hair, buying an international ticket did seem on the steep side. Another one deliberately misled me. When I followed her directions, I found myself in front of the fish market and the only person cutting anything was a fisherwoman. I walked away, very fast, and hoped that girl who thought her hairdresser was a state secret had a bad hair day.

Finally, a pretty, 'did-you-see-me-on-television?' young thing was not only thrilled that I had approached her but she also called her hairstylist Danny immediately, from her own cell phone, and fixed up an appointment for me. Assuring me that Danny was 'wunnerful', and I should 'toe-duh-lee' trust him, she breezed off, swinging her boutique bags wildly, I suspect to keep her balance on those red heels.

The appointment was in two hours. My knees started knocking against each other. Mirrors I passed showed me how good my hair was looking at the current length. But I wasn't one to be so fooled. Who wanted to be that unadventurous, stick-in-the-mud with the world's most boring haircut? Not me. Two beers down and Danny began to seem 'wunnerful'. I could image his strong hands in my hair as he snipped and snapped, giving me the most radical haircut ever. I'd never look the same again.

I tottered up to the unisex saloon, flying high and happy. Danny masterfully put me in a chair, twirled me around and as I spun dizzily, he caught the tips of my hair, hemmed, hawed, tsked, then rubbed his hands together and said, 'Okay'.

I closed my eyes after this and squawked, 'Do what you want'. Research be damned, spontaneity was the thing. And he did. Vile things were put on my scalp, and I felt I was in a gas chamber. If he was sculpting dead cells, why did it have to hurt so much? For hours I sat, going through a specialized form of medieval torture known only to modern man or more specifically to Danny. At the end of the agony, where I think parts of my brain were pulled out, he asked me to open my eyes. I opened them, weakly. He spun me around fast, the mirrors passed in a blur. I was dizzy, I couldn't spot me.

Suddenly, in a flash of truth, enlightenment dawned. That creature with straight hair was ME. Oh My God! Where had the curls gone? I couldn't tell whether I liked this (gulp) new look but it was different. Danny boomed, 'Well?' I stammered, 'It's lovely.' He smiled and gave me the ultimate compliment of my city, 'You look like a movie star'. Yes, of course, am on my way to sign up with Karan Johar.

The shocks didn't stop there. He then gave me the bill. It was half my height and the figure at the end was half my rent. I felt a cold hand stroke my back. I didn't have that kind of money. I never expected it to be this much. Do people actually spend this kind of money on HAIR? Could I ask Danny to wait till I signed my movie deal to pay this bill? I put my pride into my empty pockets and called an 'emergency' friend. He came over and paid.

Throughout the divorce, I had never asked anybody for money, no matter how broke I was and here was I extending a hand out for a haircut (bah!). It was embarrassing. My friend was amused and said that if I needed more I should ask. Looking at the bill again, he couldn't resist. With sheer disbelief, he burst out laughing and said, 'I think all the haircuts I am ever going to have in my life would never total to this much.'

I tossed my shiny new hair and thought darkly, when I become a celebrity, baby, you're definitely not getting any first day, first show tickets from me.

Trying to Look Sweet Sixteen at Terrible Thirty

My divorce was a rejection even if I was the one who had initiated it. It was almost like being put in a garbage bag and thrown out of someone's life. To climb out of this long, dark sack of rot and tell myself that I was worthy, still worthy, was a Herculean effort. Especially now, when Hercules's muscles were sagging.

The divorce filled me with the most unimaginable emotional bullshit possible. Like the absolutely prehistoric, terribly regressive and embarrassingly banal thought of not being 'able to keep the man'. Of not being a femme fatale, who twists a man around her finger and holds him there with his explicit consent. In my dating years, only one break-up had chomped up my heart. The others had been a mutual falling out or moving on. Even that big break-up felt like a minor drizzle when compared to the divorce. It doesn't matter whose fault it is. The end of a marriage is the end of the world (at least, for some time). For tomboys like me, who think kajal is a mega seduction tool, it is too cruel a blow.

I would wake up in the morning and look into the mirror. Straight, unflinching, taking in my little brown spots, the wrinkling at the eyes, the not so pink lips, the fatigue that seemed to hover around me, a permanent gloomy cloud. Going through an ugly duckling phase in your thirties is equivalent to getting chicken pox before your movie launch.

All this scrutiny resulted in the buying of an anti-wrinkle cream, and I thought that's not bad for someone who used to think sunscreen was make-up. I couldn't bear to increase the frequency to the parlour, where I went once a month. It was such a boring thing to do. The worst part was the facial. One school of thought has it that sleeping while someone pounds your body is delightful. My flesh moans in pain and usually comes out of a massage more exhausted than relaxed. But the very worst part of it is that you can't read.

Every morning, the thinking part of my head would fight valiantly with the superficial part that wanted to look 'wunnerful'. On some days, I would succeed and could completely disassociate with the outer body. On other days, it was not so easy. My father is to blame for this confusion. The first time I wore a saree, I thought I looked beautiful, girly and grown-up. My dad glanced at me preening and said, 'No matter what a monkey wears, it will look like a monkey. But if a monkey reads the right books, it won't sound like a monkey.' My poor father. He tried to teach me right. The result is that to this day a parlour visit is always calculated against the number of books I could have bought. But now this monkey was divorced and wanted to look like a swan.

At the best of times, it is difficult to fight against conditioned media imagery, stereotypical cues of beauty that are stuffed down the throat by the consumerist world. When the chips are down, it's worse. How does one still feel attractive in an obviously unyouthful body? Nothing could be done. This monkey was a bit raggedly and that was the truth. When I was with the Ex, it wasn't that I didn't think about how I looked but I had sort of accepted the imperfections, secure in the knowledge that they were loved by someone I found attractive enough to marry.

One day after the divorce, I was at the parlour and a lovely woman whizzed in. She was breathtaking, a diva. As she passed me, she complimented me on my 'fantastic skin'. My jaw hit the ground and bounced a few times, but I don't think she noticed. I heard her complain to the masseuse that her looks were gone but when she was young she had been such a 'bomb'.

Here was I, sitting in my scruffy jeans, feeling like a pill and this gorgeous creature from the gods was complimenting my skin and lamenting the lack of glow on hers. What did she want? A torch shining through her cheeks? That's when it hit me. All of us are bundles of insecurity. To get over it, there was only one solution – to be in love with me. I had to love myself, wrinkles and all. How could I judge how attractive I was? There's no universal good-looking meter that I could refer to. I was dealing with enough emotional nonsense. Did I really want to add the condition of my skin to that? I gave up on the beauty business. This was me and I liked me. If someone liked me, then he shared my good taste and I'd obviously get along fabulously with him.

While I was shedding one layer of superficiality, I discovered another – a layer of pop philosophy. An instant feel-good tablet of words. I'd read an inspirational quote or a chapter on self-help and get madly fixated on it, following what it had to say with the blindness of a believer. I would chant the words and feel them filling me with power.

It took me a long time to realize that self-help is common sense. To be happy, you had to get back to being comfortable in your own skin. It was amazing how the simplest of truths missed me by a mile in those days. I had to relearn that looking good was a feeling that only I could generate. If a man wasn't attracted to me, he was obviously the wrong man and no amount of parlour-going would fix that. I had to understand that my happiness was linked to whether my head thought I looked good. I didn't have to convince the mirror about my femme fatale charms but I had to convince the little grey box in my cranium. Once it gave the stamp of approval, the image-making, image-convoluting, image-brainwashing mechanisms could go take a flying dive into quicksand. It took some working on but today I know I'll grow old with me and never, ever divorce me.

I'm Not Older, Fatter and Slower but Wiser, Smarter and Happier

When I think of the years the divorce stole from my life, I'm not thinking of just 'those terrible years' but also the years of courtship we had. An MBA friend of mine calls it an 'opportunity cost' and though this sounds terribly clinical, it's bang on. The years when I should have been building a house, settling down with the partner, and making babies were spent battling the 'wrong man'. I didn't ask to be thirty-five, very broke, childless and thrown into the dating arena with a damaged heart and more baggage than an airline conveyor belt.

To say that it's frightening is an understatement. Every day, I'd wake up and try to rebuild my life. For the longest time, I stopped thinking of large life goals. I'd chalk out smaller achievements. Today, I won't cry. I'll not say 'Why' the whole day. I won't look at my dumber classmate on Facebook and feel bad about her 'success' and seemingly 'happy' life. Today, I'll go for a walk and not stay at home sulking. Simple steps to build the broken.

After I had achieved a level of normalcy, I began realizing with growing panic, my age and my lack of having done nothing to fix the gaping vacuum in my materialistic ownership. I had thought that I (we) had an eternity to build our life together, and that's why I didn't protect my life. He was supposed to always be there. An acquaintance of mine, I remember, had insisted on buying a house a year into the marriage and though she wasn't contributing to the loan, had asked her husband to put the place in her name. He did so cheerfully and much in love.

People may call him a fool but is there any other way to love? How can you give someone your most precious possession (yourself) and then bargain about the loose change (house, FDs, etc.). The Ex and I had decided that we wouldn't make any heavy investments, instead enjoy a bit of life. We did neither.

A woman should take care of herself. Not in the unfair way that the acquaintance I mentioned did but in terms of she should work, save and keep the tiniest bit for the rainy day. You can't predict the downpour but you can predict the ROI (Return on Investment).

People who truly loved me were kind and supportive. Friends would take me out and not let me pay the bill, surprise holidays were gifted, when my mixer went kaput and I was in tears (those days even that extra 3000 rupees was a huge blow), a friend came over with a new one. When I offered to pay, she refused to take the money. These random acts of kindness were innumerable. As were the random acts of cruelty.

People, the ones who don't care, judged me a loser. They never said it to my face but it's something I sensed. Like eyes on my back. When I'd pass them or talk to them, the echoes of loser would emanate from them and shroud me in self-worth so low that I'd have to spend an extra day to shake off that negativity.

For me, the best way to deal with these unsympathetic, bigoted, insensitive cretins was to keep away. I didn't need to fight them. I was fighting life. I had to save my energy to be positive, to write, to be happy, to learn to have fun again.

In a society like ours, success is measured by two things if you are a woman. Either by the husband with whom you have produced the mandatory two kids or if you've done exceptionally well in your career and you are making the moolah in sackfuls. I had done neither. Not only that, I had also gone and got myself the socially taboo identity of a 'divorcee'.

If I lived in a community, which didn't judge me by the materialistic possessions I had, my designation at work and who dangled on my arm, it would have been easier to move on. The middle-class I come from doesn't have the luxury of too much or too little money to be liberal. They only have enough and as a consequence they are constantly scared of losing that bit and sliding into poverty. This fear is passed on to successive generations and we store it in our hearts fearing the worst and working like rats, screwing the present to ensure a future. As a product of this thinking, how could I not take my divorce as a personal failure of gigantic proportions? For when it came to the middle-class hierarchy, I was at the lowest tier and sinking further with my 'shameless' confidence in my decisions.

I used to keep telling myself that these things didn't matter, but they do in an insidious way. It creeps under your skin and sometimes when I looked into the mirror, I would wonder if I was looking back at a loser. The only cure for it is to have fun. Yes, do things that the middle-class would never do because of their 'family' constraints.

I'd go for concerts and return home at 3 a.m. I'd trapeze off on shoestring budget holidays. As a backpacker, I could stay in motels where no 'mother' would let the 'apple of her eye' sleep. I could have friends home anytime I wanted. Being the social pariah has its advantages. There were no rules to follow. I could do anything, for nothing would be as bad as having 'broken' my marriage.

Slowly, the ones who felt sorry for me began envying me. I could see it in their eyes. They hated my life but their envy would shine through, especially when they dropped sarcastic statements like 'You don't have any responsibilities', 'It's easy for you to say be happy, have fun', 'You don't understand what sacrifice means'. They would badly crave for what I had carved out – a life that was joyous and unfettered by the mind-numbing boredom of daily life. I had finally understood that daily living can be fun but many of us get bogged down by the trivial.

Yes, the maid won't come, the milk will burn, the significant other in your life will lose their temper, the electricity bill won't be paid, but so what? Nothing stops you or me from having a blast through this.

The other blessing was that I stayed away from the place I grew up in, which had the highest concentration of people who'd judge me. Away from those extended 'family and friends', the kinds who saw me in school and college, thought that I would have a brilliant future and then saw it crash emulating the proverbial shooting star, leaving a big crater in my parents' life. It would have been much tougher to get better if I had lived in the middle of a society that loved me in this crazy, achiever-oriented way.

I was in another city, a city which gave me anonymity as I healed. If I so chose, the only judgements I had to face in this uncaring mass of humanity were my own. The only people I had to meet were friends who were my age, genuinely concerned about my personal happiness and didn't give a damn for social labels.

This city was also extremely conducive for single living. Women were safe. I could walk out at any time without a male escort. Go for movies, plays and to restaurants alone. Rent a house, get a job, live a life without an eyebrow being lifted at my lifestyle. The city didn't put a single stumbling block to me being single and for that this island of seven sisters will be my favourite place on earth.

My divorce truly gave me a second chance at life. I had to grab this opportunity and live a life I thought worthwhile. Being unhappy would mean that the narrow society I had fought had won. Their petty warnings, silly fears and tiny-minded presumptions had to be dashed to the ground, broken by the example of what my life was today.

At the end of everything, if I couldn't keep myself well and happy, nothing would matter – my decisions, the expectations of others, all would turn to fine dust in the sands of time. At the end of everything, my second chance had to be better than my first.

X

DATING
IN THE
MIDDLE AGES

Single and Ready to Nervously Mingle

My first date happened so organically that I didn't even realize it was happening. I had gone to a friend's house and there was this quiet guy in the corner. I missed him entirely for the first half of the evening. I was busy being the loud person who has just been let out of a cave and was making it my mission to be singlehandedly the life and soul of the party. I cracked jokes, laughed at witticisms, made outrageous comments, darted from group to group. After a few hours, I needed a break.

I was at the table for a refill of my cheese plate when this gentle guy sidled up to me and said, 'When you laugh, why do your eyes still look sad?' I was intrigued (total, narcissistic sucker, me) and instead of returning whence I came, I wandered across to his corner. We spent the whole evening talking. It may have seemed rude but I didn't care. Increasingly, I found conventional 'good' behaviour mighty boring. Before, I used to be the polite sheep tucking in my blackness to blend with the white, but now I zig-zagged into other pastures and the grass was definitely sweeter, especially on those obnoxious paths.

At the end of the evening, I breezily told him to call me if he was that side of town. The next day, equally breezily he said that he was going to be this side of town and would I like to do dinner. It made a challenging change from staring at my walls or reading my book, so I agreed.

I was never good at dating games. They didn't ring true. When I was young, I broke the dating rules and rewrote the book on it. If I was attracted to a guy, I asked him out; if he fancied me madly, as much as I did him, I told him. That whole 'Make him wait, let him feel insecure, don't say yes to the first date, etc.' never worked with me. I used to be so completely upfront about the whole thing that a friend of mine remarked, 'You are like a guy when it comes to dating.' I'm not sure whether that's a compliment but it saved a lot of time and meaningless analysis.

I was glad this guy had given me a whole day to prepare. I was smiling from ear to ear at office. The corporate rats were quite suspicious, constantly questioning me and making ribald statements. It's strange. If they see you gloomy and down in the dumps they think it's normal, it must be something to do with 'work', but if they see you spinning with happiness they look at it a little suspiciously, disbelieving that a human being could find so much joy at a place of work.

I didn't offer any explanations but I did take half a holiday. I told my boss, 'Don't ask me why, but please give me the second half off. I have done all my work.' Bless his grumpy old heart, he agreed and as I skipped away I could feel his smile chasing my back.

I treated myself to a good lunch and spent half my book budget on a relaxing glow massage, a fruit facial that cost more than a kilo of mangoes, strawberries and apples put together, a foot and hand spa (just like a normal pedicure or manicure except for a smelly pack they left on for half an hour) and I was ready. I had decided not to get my hair set or blow dried for I wanted to look natural.

The next three hours were spent choosing what to wear. I had to take calm breaths and stop telling myself that this was the first man I was going out with in five years. Outfits were worn and unworn. My ironed clothes were crumpled into a pile and I wailed the lament of every woman: 'I have nothing to wear'. Before I jumped off the sixth floor, I spied a gorgeous blue top.

It was superbly cut and full sleeved. My cousin had got it for me for she wanted to give me a dress which was 'modest'. The poor creature. She didn't notice the deep cowl neck the top came with. Semi-formally sexy. The exact look I wanted.

He came on time, which was a good sign, and loved the way I had done up my flat. We went to a quirky, eccentric place I had never been before. That was surprising. I thought I knew all the holes in my neck of the woods, but here was this tucked-away delightful little restaurant which served authentic Italian food.

The evening was a lyrical medley of conversation, music and delicious food. There was also interesting wine, which the guy charmingly confessed he knew 'jack' about.

I sipped my wine and saw myself reflected in the glass. That smiling girl was me spending a beautiful evening with a guy she was attracted to. There was no looming darkness at my shoulder. Life seemed normal. When the evening had started off, I wasn't sure whether I was supposed to tell him what had happened and why I was here, at this age, dating him.

In my typical fashion, I solved the quandary by asking him what I should do. He got bonus points for not looking shocked.

He shrugged it off with a 'Your history isn't important unless you feel the need to share it' and the evening began on a fresh, new note. I also learnt a very critical dating lesson.

I didn't have to go into what happened with my marriage each time I went out with a boy. All that murky business was unimportant and I could explain it away with a dignified 'It didn't work out'. I'd talk about it only to those who graduated to the tenth date, who I felt needed to know this little bit about me to understand me better, to get a better insight about where I came from.

Our waiter changed into his T-shirt and looked at us pointedly. We checked the clock. It was a half hour after closing time. Guiltily, like naughty school children who had played out too long, we called for the cheque. If only the restaurant had been open all night.

I was a bit shy about calling him home for I wasn't sure what it entailed and I didn't want to find out. I was taking baby steps in this dating world, I didn't want to start running and trip. He dropped me to my gates in a taxi, though I protested that I could walk home alone. Goodbyes done and I was walking up the stairs when my phone rang. This friend of mine, with breathless excitement, asked whether the Ex and I were together again.

Indignant, I replied in the negative. She claimed that she had seen me laughing and talking to the Ex next to the cabbie stand that night. I hung up a bit puzzled after telling her firmly that I had no intention of ever getting back with the Ex.

My thoughts wandered to the guy I went out with. He was bald and wiry like the Ex. I called a mutual friend and asked him to tell me frankly whether that guy and the Ex resembled each other. He started laughing and said that it was really weird for all of them to see me talking to that guy at the party. Apparently, he was a 'spitting image' of the Ex. My friend quite heartlessly even joked that if I hitched up with this guy nobody would believe that I had ever got divorced. It would solve all the trouble. And if I took him back home, nobody would even notice that this guy was a different one.

The penny dropped with the loudest clang. Was this a subconscious cruel trick I had played on myself? Was I not over the Ex? Am I doomed to keep finding versions of the husband-that-was-no-more, stuck in a recurring time wrap, my own personal Sci-fi movie where I was the leading star?

I was scared that night and wondered in what other ways I was fooling myself. As I hugged myself tight that night, I made a small promise. It didn't solve anything but it was a start. No more bald men. Ever.

Avoiding the Ex before the Ex

He wasn't bald. He was balding. I knew him from another life, before the Ex. The Ex before the Ex. Just as he had all those years ago, this time too he stumbled into my life in a friendly non-threatening way.

Time had passed and I had gone through an emotional turbulence that had brought about selective amnesia. I remembered only our good times. When I met him, he hadn't changed that much. The same smile, the same ease with which he interacted with the world around him, the seemingly balanced liberal viewpoint on everything. Perfect on paper, attractive in the flesh.

In the first half hour of the first meeting, our old camaraderie came back. We had always gotten along and the hiccups of meeting after so much time were almost non-existent. There were none of those normal dating irritants. At the end of the evening, cloaked in the safety net of his obvious attraction and affection, I went home to dream old dreams.

I had forgotten. His affection wasn't a safety net, it was a cocoon. You know what happens to larva inside a cocoon? It gets made into soup. No, he wasn't anything as vulgar as violent or abusive. He was worse. He was a player.

A player is a man who refuses to commit. He's there haunting our social circles and a few of us have had our hearts slightly dented by such creatures at least once. I made the mistake of being singed, twice.

Whenever I think of him, the thought, 'Those who forget history are condemned to repeat it' flashes through my head. I had forgotten why he was an 'Ex' in the first place.

He did the things he had done before. He bought lovely gifts, made the distance disappear by taking flights and coming to my doorstep. He called me every morning and night.

He didn't ever say the word 'love'. He never spoke about a future. When we were with friends, he never referred to me as anything special. He didn't make a single promise that I could hold him to.

I was caught in a whirlpool of his making and confused by such deception. He did everything a man in love would do, except say those words. I spoke to a girlfriend of mine as it was troubling me. I had to clarify whether I was reading the signs wrong or had the dating game so changed that I had no clue of how to play it. She listened. After I finished, she told me most emphatically to pick up my skirts and run. She said that there are papers written on men like that.

They lay out their traps and before we are even aware of it, we are caught in a web of waiting. We will wait for him to commit and he will continue to play this game of not doing so as long as we allow it. Finally, one day when we call his bullshit and ask him about a future, he will claim to be confused. He will want more time and that time will take so long that we will forget how much we wanted that future with him. At that point, he will convert us into a friend.

By then, we would have gotten used to him and he will constantly hang in the periphery of our life, 'always a friend, sometimes a lover'. The worst part of it is this insecure, unsure waiting for him will shut out the other men who could have walked into our lives at that point. Real men, true men, men worthy of our love.

All this she explained to me in great detail. I saw the truth and the patterns. I knew I had been saved twice from him. The first time I had to leave the city. The second time it was my friend's words, warning me about the Player.

As she advised, I called his bullshit. Like she predicted, he asked for time, trying to squirm out of it, saying that he was 'confused'. She told me that he was a textbook case and he was acting textbook. I was awestruck by the cliché playing itself out.

I thought about his women friends and came to the unsurprising conclusion that they had all dated him at some point. I immediately cut contact with him. He called, hurt. Nobody had done this to him before.

My friend had told me that I shouldn't engage in drama and tell him firmly that we both wanted different things in life and therefore should go our separate ways. He tried once more to save what he called a 'friendship'. I cruelly told him that I had enough friends.

He kept trying after that but I was firm. I didn't want to be played anymore. He taught me another important lesson. Before I got into the dating game again, I had to be clear about what I wanted. Did I want to get remarried? Or did I need a relationship? Did I still believe in marriage? Or did I not want to think about any of these things and want to float for a bit and enjoy myself?

The reason I wanted this clear in my head wasn't for me but for the person I would be going out with. I didn't want to be a player. I thought any man I dated should understand my emotional requirements. I didn't want to lead anybody on or imply a false future when none existed. The Player, in fact, ironically defined who I would be in the whole dating arena. He taught me that I needed to keep a code of conduct in order not to hurt people while I meandered through this emotional chaos.

Thank god for my girlfriend. Meeting the Ex before the Ex and what followed next lasted a mere four months. After I kicked him out of my life, it took me one day to get over his deception. I had come out of something that had cost me five years of my life. What he did was as inconsequential as a mosquito bite, forgotten the next day.

Even today, I feel this spring of happiness bubble in me when I think of how I escaped his clutches. The more I live, the more I am convinced of this fact. Irrespective of gender, each and every one of us deserves someone who will love us truly with honesty. I would like to be with someone who will think of me as the most important asset in their life. If anybody makes an excuse not to be with me, I must have the good sense to understand that he doesn't want to. This fact is so simple it takes away my breath. I'd like to be with someone who will love me like the way I love them.

The Frogs' Brigade

The bald man and the Player were put up on the 'To avoid' list and I thought I was safe. Hah! The minute the universe knew I was single, it started rounding up the frogs it knew, the ones who didn't turn into a prince, and began sending them my way. Forget prince, they didn't even turn into a nice banking clerk.

They came into my life drawn by unforeseen forces, these people who had such huge chinks that the human being in them seemed missing in action. I wasn't asking for perfection. But I was hoping at least for a 'Let's have a normal time'. That, in this shockingly dysfunctional world of ours, comes at a premium. Let me introduce you to the frogs I met.

The Married Man

Though I refer to this person in singular, it's actually in plural. Married men began crawling out of the woodwork as soon as they knew of my divorced status and started wooing me with a sickening creepiness. I knew their wives. They were such interesting women and would have had the guy's balls for breakfast if they knew what was happening.

It is a logical truth that anybody single who is in an affair with a married man is an idiot who is being used. This sounds harsh but it is the truth. The guy gets the best of whatever worlds he wants, while the women wait. The wife when he is with her. She, when he is with his wife. And yet, at least two people I know are sitting in this cage of being 'used' and waiting patiently, throwing away their life on this utterly worthless man who is a waste of space, time and energy. The women have painted themselves into a corner and all they need to do to find their happiness is walk out or, better still, throw him out. Instead, they choose to simmer at the violation of their core, without taking any concrete action, and fritter away the goodness they have on an ass whose value system is totally skewed to suit his convenience.

The scary part was that the married men who hit on me were interesting, funny, charming people, the sorts I would have loved to be married to. They didn't come with an aura of being jerks, but their actions were despicable. How does one know the man you are with is a decent bloke when all around you faith is broken and trust is compromised?

It was a tough balancing act. I didn't want to be perceived as a virginal touch-me-not, neither did I want to lead a married man on and get into a situation I couldn't get out of. I had a few rules to help me.

Unless the man was an old friend, I never hung out with married men alone.

If a man, especially colleagues, casual acquaintances, started bitching about his wife, I discouraged him.

I assumed nothing till they made an explicit move and then with equal clarity I told them where they could go and shove their cheating selves.

I had learnt to deal with an adult world that was messy and opportunistic. I had honed myself to be extra vigilant. And between being cool or cautious, I always chose cautious.

The Runner

I used to adore these sorts in college and my friends would be perpetually scared I'd marry one of them. They were fascinating creatures but could never be counted on. One of them drifted into my life during this time. I had the most madcap evening. He took me to the flower market and we watched tonnes of coloured, vibrant florals being loaded, unloaded, sorted and carried away. Visually, it was a spectacle and as a date it was spectacular.

After that feast of colours, we walked home as he had said it was a lovely night to stroll. Suddenly, a car stopped beside us. Without warning, he began running away from the car, away from me. With a thundering heart I wondered what would happen next. Nothing did, they merely wanted directions. After the car drove off, he came back and casually asked what they wanted. Equally casually I enquired why he felt like jogging at that particular moment. He brushed it off saying that it wasn't important. I didn't dig deeper for an explanation, a bit wary of what I might uncover. My radar was fine-tuned and I knew here was a person with strange wiring in his head, which I didn't have the energy for. At my apartment gate, he pointed at a mermaid in the moon. She was pretty but he was history.

The Assorted Odd Ones

The Floater – At forty, he was still looking for meaning in life and carried the angst of a teenager as the fire of his integrity. This type wants a babysitter, not a girlfriend.

The Square – He had lived too long in a routine he had perfected. He had no room for your eccentricities. If you wanted to share his life, you'd have to become a square – his square with the exact same dimensions. A millimetre more and he'd hammer you back into the right dimension – at your cost.

The Workaholic – He is scared. Suddenly and desperately, he feels he has missed out on love as he was too busy working. This fear will drive him to date but he can't stop working. The only time he has for a relationship is at night, when the office sleeps. If I was an insomniac this may have been a pleasant diversion.

The Bore – There is nothing wrong with him, but my rule of thumb is that if you get bored on the first date, how can you bear a lifetime? If you don't want to run, practise yawning discreetly.

There are many other kinds. Luckily, I didn't meet all of them but I have heard the stories. The world of dating is incredibly scary with the number of lunatics on the prowl. This isn't a gender thing. I think for the number of cuckoo men there are, there are an equal number of loopy-in-the-unfun-way women. Sometimes, the pairing itself doesn't work. As in, a particular person will work badly only with this other particular person. With someone else they may be fine. The permutations and combinations of things that can go wrong when you are looking for that perfect mate is so frightening, it's best not to think about it.

In a sense, there is no protection, no guide book. As a single person who doesn't want to be alone, the only way to go through this is to go through this. The divorce had taught me many things and one of them was a finer understanding of who I was and what I wanted. I had to be true to my heart, my principles and what I desired. Beyond that, nothing else was in my control. I had to cross my fingers and hope that lady luck would be a lady with me. This time.

Candlelight Dinner over a Mouse

The real world of men wasn't working. I hadn't met a single man who I thought may even make a worthwhile acquaintance, forget about one who qualified for the partner bit. That's when I decided to go online.

I come from a slightly dated dating school. Here, people I know would introduce me to people they know. This way, the person comes with a certificate of decency (or so I thought). At least, they wouldn't turn out to be cannibalistic serial killers. At the most, they may have insane politics or there wouldn't be any chemistry. Simple things that I could deal with.

I felt Victorian when I decided to go online and see if I could find my elusive partner. Trepidation, stomach catches and pure fear fuelled every click. I was petrified to say the least. A friend suggested that I go for an expensive paid site for the 'riff-raff' wouldn't be there. I knew money was no guarantee of anything. Having ignored the advice, I was wondering what to do. Randomly Googling, I stumbled across two articles on online dating in the New Yorker.

I looked them up and they did have an India chapter. I registered myself without a picture and surname. I didn't want my friends to find me there (at this point, I was immature and thought that online dating was a desperate move. It isn't and the only people who feel this way are the ones who aren't comfortable with the changing world). In my antiquated circles, this would have been such a 'loser' thing to do. In fact, more 'loser' than getting a divorce. (Often, it occurs to me that my world hasn't moved outside the college definition of 'cool'.)

The one thing that struck me while going through the profiles is that a fantastic person with poor writing and vocabulary skills would fail in these sites. If their left brain was stronger than their right, there's no way they would find a partner in this world of superficial impressions and magical words that have to cast the first spell.

(A gossipy, spiteful aside. When I was looking through profiles, I came across 'The Player'. Remember him? His profile said that he was interested in 'pole dancing' among other things. I laughed and laughed, thinking of his chubbiness hugging a long, lean pole.)

After searching copiously, I narrowed down on two people. They were both in my city, divorced and seemed to have a funny side. Also, I must confess snobbishly, their education was quite impeccable.

While looking through the site, I remembered an uncle of mine. His daughter was having the most difficult time in her arranged marriage. I was one of the few people he would speak to. Once with tears in his eyes, he asked me what he could have done to have avoided this fate for his daughter. He had checked the man's family, education and providing power. What more could he do? How could the poor man fathom what his daughter would find interesting and attractive? How could he gauge that man's caring quotient (one of her grouses was that the guy would order pizza for himself without checking whether she wanted any)? The daughter divorced the man and had another arranged marriage. I can only imagine Uncle's trepidation and fear as he chose the second one and admire the girl's courage (or should I despise her cowardice?) for letting him make that decision for her, again.

After we exchanged emails, I decided to meet one of the guys. Like an idiot, I gave him my address and then sat in a sweat for the next three days wondering if he was a psycho. I bought an extra can of pepper spray. I had two now, one for each room, but if he attacked me in the kitchen, I was doomed. He came that Friday and rang the doorbell. I practised reaching out for the pepper spray, kept strategically at an arm's length and opened the door.

He had gentle, green eyes. I never knew, the photos didn't show that. We got talking and it was pleasant, effortless. The only weird bit was that he said that he wanted water (no, that wasn't the weird bit. Patience). I walked to my fridge to get it. I bent down, took out the water bottle and when I turned around, there he was, right behind me peering at what's in the fridge. It spooked me, he moved with the tiptoe finesse of a cat burglar.

During dinner we spoke very little about relationships but more about books, music and movies. It was a happy evening. We had similar values and we didn't ruffle each other with our viewpoints. However, at the back of my head, 'You don't know him, You don't know him, You don't know him, You don't know him,' kept being chanted.

Post dinner (he paid for it, and I joked that if he kept paying for all the people he would meet online, he'd go broke very soon and wouldn't have any money to get married), we stepped out of the restaurant and I was wondering what to do next.

He suggested a midnight ice cream. I agreed and immediately regretted it. Sitting in his car, my eyes noted that the door wasn't locked. He drove masterfully, with an ease and confidence that is sexy in a man. Once we got to the ice cream place, I relaxed. I don't mind being in the open with a stranger. It was effortless, this being with him, licking our ice creams, laughing at small jokes, two people whose pitch was in tune.

Just then we saw a large procession singing songs and walking towards a destination purposefully in the middle of the night. They were dressed in dance costumes and were crooning in a language neither of us knew. In my five years in Bombay, I had never seen a procession that was so colourfully creative. Neither had he.

He looked at me with shining eyes and asked whether we should join them, follow them and see what happens. Normally, I would have skipped along. But the fear came back. I said next time, and when he dropped me home, I quickly took the lift and didn't invite him in.

I am not sure whether it was a move but he said he wanted to use the loo. Now my heart was doing a drum roll. I let him into the house. He used the loo and came out. I blurted out that I didn't want to kiss him. He looked surprised and said, 'Of course'. Yes, it was the most natural thing to not want to kiss him. He left promising to call again.

He did, but by then I knew I couldn't date a person who came through these channels. I had to do it the old fashioned way. I couldn't let myself go. I'd always be scared that I was being fooled. That my judgement was being shaped. That's when it hit me. I'm an 'arranged-marriage' type. The difference is that my friends arrange it for me and not my parents or extended family. I never called the second guy even though he had sexy oxfords, and that too, the right shade of brown.

Firing Prince Charming

'What sort of guy do you want?' How many times have I have answered this question. In my youth, how many revised and re-revised lists have I made with all the characteristics of the 'perfect man'. What a bumbling, naive fool I was. Today, what I want from a man has changed so much, he is almost unrecognizable as Prince Charming.

Today:

He can keep the toilet seat up, down or even pull it out with his bare hands. I don't care if he leaves his towel / jeans / shorts / himself on the floor. He can drop whatever he wants and be the king of clumsiness as long as he picks me up when I am down.

He doesn't have to give me a back massage, a toe massage, a bubble bath surprise. He just shouldn't mangle my heart.

He can listen to rap, acid rock, trance and all the other music I don't get. I will not say a word as my ears get assaulted by the screeching noises of bands I avoid. He can hate my classic rock and jazz. He can make fun of Pink Floyd and think Dylan is a wuss. It won't matter as long as he doesn't make fun of me, maliciously.

He doesn't have to buy me those deep red flowers, woo me with candlelight dinners, drown me in sudden, intense gifts or kidnap me to surprise romantic destinations if only he will be kind to my parents, hold me when I am scared and respect my mood swings without dismissing me.

He doesn't have to leap before me, run ahead with barely concealed enthusiasm and fling open the door before my dainty hand touches the handle, as long as he doesn't slam the door shut on my face.

He can create an entire orchestra with his snoring through the night. I will not poke him in the ribs, complain loudly about it to the neighbours or go sleep in another room. As long as his decibel levels don't increase while he is talking to me.

He doesn't have to fix a flat, fight with gangsters, ride stallions or do a solo cruise across the seas to bring back a scarf I dropped. He just has to be aware about what's important to me and respect that enough to help me make it come true in my life.

He can play with the mobile, the computer, the Xbox, the Play Station, the video game as long as he wants and as many hours as he wants. My only request is that he doesn't play games with my heart.

He doesn't have to leave secret notes under the pillow or write me love poems in blank verse. Instead, I'd be more than happy if he files his taxes and plans his investment.

I don't need an our song, our table, our restaurant, our dance move. I just need an us.

I'd rather he didn't carve our initials on a tree or a stone or a bridge, by hanging upside down, fifty feet from the water, causing me a mild heart attack. Instead, he needs to make sure that his signature on the cheques is the right one so that they don't bounce, especially when they are half-the-rent cheques.

He doesn't have to tell me 'I love you' a million times in rote, the way he repeated his mathematical tables. Instead, if he said it once, meant it and never forgot that he meant it, what more can I ask for?

We don't need to watch sunsets together as long as he'll watch my eyes and figure out when I am hurt or wipe away the tears.

He doesn't have to dance with me in the kitchen as long as he doesn't push me against a wall.

I don't care if he kisses me goodnight but when he kisses me, he must kiss like he means it and not as if he is dusting a fly off his lip.

He doesn't have to tell me he will never cheat on me a hundred million times, he just has to be faithful in action.

I don't need him to come to the temple with me. But he shouldn't insult my god and if I want him to, he must have the largesse to stand at my place of worship, without the belief but with the respect accorded to another's faith.

It's okay if he doesn't like my friends as long as he doesn't insult them and welcomes them home without a twitch of irritation.

He doesn't have to cook for me but he shouldn't starve me of affection.

I will love his sense of humour as long as it isn't used as a weapon against me.

I don't need him to hold hands. I need him to hold my heart and promise not to drop and break it.

He needn't dream about me every night as long as he guards my dreams.

There is no need for him to slay dragons, defeat witches and wake me up from a cursed sleep. I can do that by myself. I need him to be there, cheering me on as I chop the dragon's neck, defeat the witch and wake up by myself fighting the sleeping potion with inner strength.

Today, I don't want a Prince Charming. Neither do I want a Prince Heartbreaker, Prince Sorrow Sharpener, Prince Hate Gardner, Prince Lie Generator, Prince Backbone Cutter, Prince Time Stealer.

Today, all I want is Prince Good to Me.

XI

AND SHE LIVED HAPPILY EVER AFTER

What I Did on Meeting the Ex on a Dark, Lonely Road

I wonder when the Ex will stop being a part of my life. Maybe never or maybe someday when his importance in shaping my life is diminished by another force that will fashion it with love instead of hurt.

A friend of mine called most concernedly when I sent her a forward. She enquired with breathless agitation why I had also marked the Ex on it. I told her as politely as I could that it was a topic he'd also be interested in (for the reader who is curious about these little things, it was about cycling in the Black Forest). She hung up quite angry, with variations of 'After all he has done' explained in painful detail and varying pitches. I listened with half an ear, she wouldn't get it.

The Ex wasn't evil. As strange as it sounds, other than breaking up the marriage he hadn't done anything else that was despicable. We had reached a quiet camaraderie these days. He'd call occasionally asking about my health and happiness. When there was a concert I'd love to attend, he'd pick up extra tickets. Like an old couple, who knew each other, too well, too long, we'd go together for it. Once when I was particularly unhappy, he came home with a gift of books.

I fully understood what he meant to me when a large crisis loomed in office. There was a possibility that my department would be annexed. I was not unduly scared, though it meant that I may have to give up my house. I hadn't saved enough to have a safety net.

That's when I knew that my safety net was the Ex. If at any point I had nowhere to go, I knew I could walk into the house we had shared once. Whether I would actually do so or not is a moot point. The crisis solved itself and my job, at least for now, remains intact.

I'll never forget that feeling, how with a blinding clarity, I sensed that the only house I could live in on charity would be that of the Ex. Was it because I still felt a connection with him or was it because he was a genuinely decent guy? I will leave it to the shrink I refused to see to figure it out.

I once asked the Ex what he felt for me now that everything had been tied up in strings and filed away. He said nothing, instead tears welled up in his eyes. That damn silence came again between us and settled its fat, quiet ass. I gave up. Why do I even try?

As I began dating, occasionally I'd see him walking down the street. I would introduce him and the two men would say hello, shake hands and chat awhile. I'd marvel at this Julian Barnes life I was leading. I had become a character in one of those dysfunctional books I read.

One particular birthday of the Ex, he asked me whether I'd accompany him to a concert. I refused as I already had a previous commitment and I was going to the concert with that person.

Was this cruel on my part? I am not sure but it was needed, to move on, to survive. I had put my life on hold for him enough, no more of that. Feeling only an ant prick of guilt, I dolled up. Well, it was a date.

As Buddy Guy rocked with the raunchiness and zest for life that only a supremely talented eighty-year-old man with the good fortune of still being able to perform could have, I saw my date beside me lightly swaying to the music, intensely listening to the thing that makes us believe that life is worth it. To the right, my eye caught the Ex, alone with a beer, smiling at the magic of this man. The birthday gift he had given himself, the one I had refused to be a part of. As sadness, sharp and stinging pierced me, I felt hands on my shoulder. The date had found an armrest.

That touch reminded me why I was here, away from the Ex for I wanted the truth of someone who genuinely wanted to be with me and loved me without compromise. The sinking feeling immediately raised itself and turned into a happy bubble in my throat. I raised my beer, caught the Ex's eye and toasted him a happy birthday. We rocked together, separately but in tandem.

At the end of the concert, my date had the good manners to wish the Ex a happy birthday. I had mentioned the fact in passing and he had the generosity to remember it. It made me feel good. This show of civilization between the men I knew.

As more and more time flowed, there'd be days when I didn't think of the Ex. He was almost like a person who had died. Not there, but a clinging, fading memory. In time, the days turned into months. I must admit, though, I still haven't gone a year without thinking of him.

I consciously began refusing the concert tickets and stopped meeting him altogether. I had to train myself. If another crisis popped up, the Ex mustn't be the one I should turn to. The familiarity of the Ex had to be amputated from my life. In the beginning, it was a conscious effort. Slowly, it became a barely noticeable habit, like locking the door. To give him credit, he understood my need to close contact and respected it enough to keep away.

We had kindness between us now. Though I must say, all the acts of generosity were from him. I continued to stubbornly not engage. I wouldn't be mean to him but I couldn't be his friend. Every time he'd ask me out, I'd politely refuse. However, if he called, down about a thing only I would understand because of our history, I'd listen. My act of kindness to him was that I would never cut him when he reached out to me. That was all I could do, and on some days even that felt beyond the call of duty.

I am confident, however, that if I met him on a dark, lonely road, I'd say hello. He'd walk me a part of the way for he wouldn't want me to navigate the darkness alone. When we'd come to the light, he'd stop. Maybe we'd exchange a sentence or two before we part. Then we'd walk away from each other towards wherever we were going. He wouldn't mind letting me go now, for he would see that the road is lit.

Thank God, No Likes for My New Status

If you are active on social media, the pain of a divorce is amplified multi-fold. It amounts to hiring an auto, a loudspeaker and going around town informing the 'public' about the dissolution of your marriage. Your wall and album is probably full of pictures of the Ex, right from your dating days to the married ones, all with countless likes and tags.

During the divorce and a year after that, I had things to think of other than social media. My mind was functioning at bare minimum capacity and all it could do was focus on survival. As I was wandering through this fog, I got a message from the Ex's friend. She asked why he had dropped off the earth and whether things were okay with him. That's when I realized that on social media we still looked like we were a couple. There were snaps of us looking into each other's eyes, smiling at random things, pretend-hugging, kissing. It was quite nauseating, not to mention heartbreaking. As I went through the pictures, posts and shares that involved both of us, I remembered the incidents surrounding them.

How we both had bunked work and left on an impromptu holiday in the hills in the rainy season. We had been playing in a tiny waterfall en route on the side of the road, when a group of drunks staggered up to us. We were terrified. Six of them reeking of the local hooch. One of them leered with the absolute innocence of those caught up in a good time of their own and asked us to take a photograph of the group. Fearfully, we obliged. The Ex then cheerfully asked them to stand with us and suggested a photograph with all of us. I remember simmering at him for prolonging this interaction with those drunken beasts. After the photos, they were off. The Ex explained weakly that he thought being friends with them would have averted any danger. I rolled my eyes and tried to forget about it. Irrespective of this incident, we had a great time. The next we heard of these guys was when one of them tagged us. As I was untagging myself from this picture, a silent shiver ran through my back. I felt we had escaped a calamity, while I'm sure the Ex with his goofy grin still thinks that this wayside friendship was the most natural occurrence. I can't help tearing up looking at the innocence of our smiles, our belief in ourselves as a team, standing together cheerfully with what we thought was danger.

There was this particular photo of him running in his undies. I had clicked it and put it up as a joke. He was mortified, being a shy type, but I think after that series of snaps he got over whatever inhibition he had. He never even thanked me for this lovely little character-building I gave him.

There's another snap of me sitting in front of a tall glass of Mai Tai while he is lacing his boots to go for a hike. On one of our holidays, I had decided hiking was too much work and that this was supposed to be a vacation. I wanted to sit and chill in the cottage by the river, soak in nature and not sweat it out on a mountain. The Ex disagreed and after much grumbling he decided to go on his own. He almost got killed on that hike.

When he came back he told me his adventures, deliberately underplaying the danger. I understood and didn't nag him. He was proud of what he had achieved. I sent a quick prayer up, thanking the powers for keeping him safe. He joked that if I had come along, my clumsiness would have surely killed him. It made me smile, those memories of fear and amusement and for a split second it seemed as though almost nothing had happened after that holiday. Smiles frozen in a snap.

Of all the photographs, one of the toughest to delete was the one of two children. They embodied the nursery rhyme, with their rosy cheeks, dimpled chins and bright sparkling eyes. We had seen them on the road when we were walking, talking, in love with each other and our lives together.

We were about to cross the road when these kids came running up to us and asked for money. The Ex on an impulse decided to buy them ice creams. The four of us ate dripping ice creams, happy at the unexpected treat and watched the setting sun, marvelling at the surprises of the day. Before we said goodbye, the Ex took snaps of those children and promised me that someday we'd have two of our own. I remember carrying the thought in my heart and how it had warmed me the whole week. Whenever we spotted those kids, we'd look at each other and smile. Over time, the kids disappeared, as street kids do with frightening regularity.

Deleting snaps one by one was getting increasingly difficult. Memory after memory would spring up like helpless pieces of floating paper and I'd be carried into painful memory pockets I thought I didn't have in me anymore.

There was much I had to do – edit my status, untag myself and delete those photographs and conversations. After three hours, I had just trawled through the first year. There were four more years to delete, to wipe out, to pretend they never happened.

I didn't think my heart could survive going through all of them. If I did, I'd probably be found the next morning in a pool of salt water. Is 'death due to crying' a valid medical possibility? I wasn't keen to find out.

The other fact that was making me feel a bit queasy was that if I changed my status to 'single' I couldn't predict people's reactions to it. My close friends and a splattering of acquaintances in Bombay knew. What about school and college friends? Mothers of these friends? Ex-colleagues in different cities. It seemed as if I would spend the rest of my life answering questions about my status update.

I didn't want to go through the gamut of sympathy/support/commiseration and love that would flood in. This kind of grief is personal and is best kept that way. Also, social media comments have a way of being completely banal and predictable. I didn't want to hear things straight out of a Hallmark card, which would make me squirm, grit my teeth and break the computer.

I stumbled on a solution, which I'm sure is the least technology friendly one. I copy-pasted my friends' names on a word document. I saved the solo pictures I was vain about, which didn't include the Ex or our times together and then I deactivated my account. It was better than going through the timeline in great detail.

The next weekend I opened a new account, put up the photographs that had been carefully sieved out and sent out friend requests to the people on my wordlist. I judiciously avoided those who had been introduced to me or came into my life via the Ex. It almost felt like I was creating a new life and a new identity for myself. A life where a person called the 'Ex' never existed. Maybe, in time, that's how it will be. He will be completely erased from my life. And here's a like for that thought.

How Feminism Saved Me Paperwork

It is true we don't choose our names. If we did most of us wouldn't be called what we are. When my parents named me, they were obeying a four-year-old. My cousin was staying with us at the time I was born. When they brought me home, a wee defenceless bundle who didn't comprehend what 'protest' meant, they wanted to include him in the grand event. They asked his opinion on what I should be named. At that point, he was in nursery and he had a crush on a girl called Arathi.

Needless to say, that was the name he most enthusiastically suggested. My mother tried not listening to him and suggested a more musical Radhika. He threw a temper tantrum and howled the roof down. As a result, I got one of the most common names in south India. The cousin forgot about the incident, till one day, during a family dinner, my mom revealed his role in my nomenclature. He still hasn't apologized.

I have met more Arathis than I can count. I have four very close friends who go by the same name. When we call each other we call ourselves. Leaving messages always leads to giggles and clichéd jokes.

Every class I was in had at least three to four Arathis. Teachers to differentiate us would call us by our full names. They were kind in those days and refrained from telling us apart with cruel descriptions. For example, the Arathi who picks her nose or the Arathi who smells a bit funny or the Arathi who comes last in running. No, they were very gentle. I was called Arathi Menon – luckily it was a short name and they didn't mind. Unlike Arathi Parathaswamy Iyengar. One teacher gave up and began calling her Partha, which soon caught on. We still refer to her as Partha.

I think this is one of the reasons when I think of myself, I think of my full name. I asked my friends and a lot of them said that they identify with only their first name, as their surname was what belonged to their family. Therefore, changing it after marriage was not a big deal. Perhaps, if I was called Arathrika, I'd think of myself, and quite grandly I must say, in the first name too.

The day I got married, my uncle solicitously enquired whether I'd be changing my name. I told him 'Maybe'. This wasn't an act of rebellion; it was how I had thought of myself all these years. To suddenly truncate my name and attach another surname to it would have been weird. Like undergoing cosmetic surgery and seeing someone else in the mirror.

I think I was also suffering from a college hangover. The feminism I had read there had seeped down too deeply to let me take a man's name. (It, of course, didn't protect me from taking a man's bullshit.) Germaine Greer, Erica Jong, Simone De Beauvoir, Virginia Woolf, Naomi Wolf and a horde of other women had spent their thinking years, their lives, teaching me how to carve my own identity. I owed it to them to keep my name and not let a man change what they had drummed in was my exclusive identity.

In certain cultures in India, a woman's name is changed after she gets married. If that had happened to me, I'm sure I would have spent my whole life not answering anybody's calls. For I simply wouldn't remember my new name.

The Ex didn't have an opinion one way or the other. He didn't want me to romantically take his name to be his. He told me clearly that it was my choice and he didn't care. The only suggestion he made was that maybe I could keep my surname and add his, with a hyphen. It sounded very French.

I felt this was a good option. I agreed in theory to take the Ex's name. However, in practise since we were both lazy urban rats, we never got around to going to the office and getting my name officially changed. Who wants to spend a Saturday, a holiday, in a government office? We'd rather have a scrumptious toss-up lunch and lounge, resting our tired working cells.

Thank god, I kept my maiden name for imagine the bureaucratic headache I would have to go through to change it back after the divorce. Surprisingly, by a sheer dint of luck none of my documents said I was married except, of course, the marriage certificate.

My parents are responsible for this bit of fortune. Being an only child, they made sure since the day I was born that all my state identities were in order. I was the only person I knew who had every single document the state bestows on its citizen – birth certificate, passport, PAN card, Aadhar card, voter identity card, ration card, driving licence. They were lovingly arranged in a file by my overanxious father, who used to take colour photocopies of them and send me the copy. Wisely, they didn't trust their child with the originals of these important documents.

Most of my friends had to go and get these things themselves. My parents have stood in queue for hours to ensure that I was counted as a citizen of the country. When I got married, I let these identity proofs remain. Oddly, my parents didn't show the same zeal to convert any of these documents into ones that also established my marital status.

Marriage and the breaking up of it is such an emotionally tangled web, I was glad I didn't have to add any legal tangles to it. A friend of mine had kept her married name after the divorce. She said it was easier, she didn't want to take the effort to change it again.

I remembered when she had gotten married she was furious with her then husband because he wanted her to take his name. He had convinced her that it was an act of love and not ownership. So she was saddled with a name she didn't want imposed on her by a man who was no more at her side.

As a birthday gift, I got her the papers she needed to change her name back to the one she had started her life with, before him. A period when she was less cynical and looking at the world without having undergone pain. She broke down when she saw my gift. She showed me a book which was filled with her signature spelling out her maiden name. She confessed that when she was depressed she'd go on a signing bout. It was definitely cheaper than seeing the shrink. Today, she has her own name, the one her parents gave her and nothing on earth will make her change that. Especially, not another man.

What I Learnt from the Ex

The skies came holding their clouds and the greys washed over the city. I got a call from the Ex and having nothing better to do, I joined him for an evening of watching the harbour show off its water colour moods.

It was one those contemplative days and I asked him whether he wanted to give me any advice which I could use, if and when I decided to be with someone else again. He squirmed and showed great reluctance to exercise his mind in this fashion. I persisted.

The first point he said was, 'Don't think you are always right'. We had both gone beyond anger and I earnestly, out of genuine curiosity, asked him when I had said something that had turned out to be wrong.

He began with a confident 'So many times' and as he started thinking of 'those times', I saw him get distinctly uncomfortable. He shifted in his chair in a hundred small ways. If I didn't know him well, I'd think he had mosquitoes under his bum. He hemmed and hawed but came up with nothing concrete. Too much sorrow had shrouded our world for me to feel smug, but I did sense a teeny-weeny triumphant glow and allowed myself a discreet smile.

He took it with good grace. He grinned and said, 'Maybe

you were always right but it was mighty annoying.' Point taken. That evening I went back home and thought about what this experience with the Ex had taught me. These are his lessons, which I haven't forgotten.

Be Unafraid: I learnt to fear nothing. I had discovered immense bravery and self-reliance in me. I had streams, rivers and oceans of strength, and they would hold me when I broke down without anybody's help.

Chase Happiness: We're all going to die. This time I have on earth, I owe it to myself to be happy. I can crib and cry about trivialities, the computer crashed or my boss is an asshole. The truth is, every day, I am immensely lucky to be healthy, to be sane, to have a shot at doing something with this life I have been generously given.

Learn to Save: Men will come and go. Bank balances if watched over and taken care of will stay and grow. Money through a job brought me freedom, self-respect and the power to start over again.

Keep Friends: When I was in a relationship I forgot my friends. Luckily for me, they were the understanding sort who came when I was broken, forgetting that I had ignored them. I also learnt to sieve the good friends from the bad. Nothing is as much an acid test of friendship as bad times. The ones who stay are the ones who are worth it. The rest is a waste of time and space in your heart.

Forgive: If I continued to hate the Ex or harboured negativity about him, it meant that I was still carrying him within me. I had to learn to be neutral towards him. To treat him with the common compassion I'd give any living being. Once I began to do that, he stopped dominating my mind and slowly began to erase himself from me.

Have Faith: There are innumerable acts of goodness happening to us every second, right from the man who braked while I crossed the road dangerously to my colleague who saved a piece of her daughter's birthday cake for me. We must have faith in that. There's a line in Woody Allen's *Manhattan*, where this young girl tells him, 'You have to have a little faith in people'. I must get these words tattooed on my arm.

Don't Lose the Good Parts: Before I met the Ex and during the relationship when I was happy, there were many things about me that were good. I took extra care to retain those bits of me. I didn't want to come out worse from this muck than I had gone in. I owed that to myself.

Be Proud: A large number of people whom I have met, who have gone through a divorce, feel an acute sense of shame. Even I do occasionally, but it is extremely important not to let anybody even get a whiff of it. It's the society we live in, making the victim feel the guilt. As long as I hold my head high, nobody can do a damn thing about it. It's only when I am weak that they will prey with their morality.

Believe: Nobody else needs to believe in me if I do. The only guarantee I have in life is myself. Luckily for me, as I came from parents who reiterated that I was worthy of love every waking moment, it was easy for me to relearn this. My divorce was a rejection of me. To get over that, I had to accept all of me - flaws, dents, quirks, eccentricities and even the not-so-nice parts.

Dissolve Boxes: My only limit is myself. It inspires me that every day I wake up to a brand new twenty-four hours. During this time, I can change whatever I don't like about myself, act in a way that will get me a step closer to achieving what I want. The grumpiness and depression I felt yesterday belongs to yesterday, the past. One of my greatest achievements is that I am not in limbo. I'm moving, constantly towards various kinds of fulfilments. This in itself is worth the pain.

Every day is a step forward in this new life I am creating. Every day is the hope I saw during those dark times. Every day is a gift I've earned because I had the courage to demand more from this world.

You must be wondering why I am giving credit to the Ex for these lessons. If the divorce hadn't happened, I would still be living a world of make-believe, with the innocence of 'my-husband-bestest-and-will-take-care-of-me-forever'.

It is painful for me to admit that I am used to having someone look after me whether it was parents, boyfriends or husbands. To actually move away from that, to be truly independent in spirit and in behaviour took me thirty-five years. On the brighter side, it didn't take me seventy.

Trusting the L Word Again

After you go through a divorce, there are two choices. One is you decide to keep away from the dreaded word – love. It is the biggest risk you take as an adult and you think it is advisable to follow this capricious emotion with caution. You know it is the only thing in the world that can mangle your happiness into an unrecognizable form. You swear never again will another human being have this much power over you. You vow that from now on your heart will be kept under lock, key and strict surveillance. No matter how great the temptation or how wonderful a heart-stealer can seem, you will scrupulously avoid him and stick to safe zones.

Or you can be like me. I figured nothing could hurt me so much ever again. No matter what happened to me, I would survive. I had proved beyond doubt the depth of my inner strength to myself. Therefore, what was I scared of? Love? Nah. This love can come and sweep me off my feet. I will ride it with the confidence of the world. For if it comes crashing down, I can pick me up again. This time, I'm sure it will be faster for I've had practise.

Isn't it crazy that breaking down a marriage makes me want to have another? When I married the Ex, I did it to please my mum.

She thought I was definitely over the hill and threw adequate temper tantrums and piled high the emotional blackmail that I fell into line. Kicking, screaming but smiling for the wedding photograph.

However, now that I had had a taste of coupledom it seemed quite delectable. I think what was partially to blame was when it was good with the Ex it was very good and when it was bad it was still bearable. The other factor, which made me want to trust love again, is that I knew some incredibly wonderful men. By being supportive, funny, loving and, occasionally, giving me a swift kick on my 'poor-me' butt, they taught me not to hate men. They helped me believe in people who could have a strong moral code and an inner core of such strength; it was a privilege to associate with them. I wanted someone like that in my life for it would make me richer. It would fill my world with colours I couldn't paint myself.

The next question was where do I find this love. I decided to be open to everything, I had nothing to lose. I went on blind dates, I met people and I learnt all sorts of things. Not all the men I met were nice but since I had gotten addicted to happiness I was unstoppable. I looked without fear and believed I would get what I wanted. I didn't make it my focus. Happiness was my focus. If I was alone, I'd be happy in my solitary garden.

Preferably, I would find someone to love for I had so much to give. It had come from my parents. They, by example, had taught me how to love generously, selflessly, effortlessly. How could I be selfish and waste this beautiful gift just on myself?

It wasn't easy to feel this need, this gaping cavity in me. The first step was to accept the need, the craving. I told my friends about it. Varied responses came my way, from the very encouraging, 'You'll find who you want' to the cynical 'All the good men are taken'. It didn't matter. I had put this wish out there and it would come when it would.

After all what is love? Do I even have the courage to answer that question? I have no idea. What I am sure of is that in spite of the things that have happened, when love comes calling, I will listen and maybe, I will follow. We who want to drink the lees of life have to be stupid that way.

In a sense, I think a divorcee is a romantic and maybe the greatest believer in marriage. Go ahead, laugh. But we are the believers for we dared to question an imperfect love and broke it for it wasn't perfection. We had the faith that there was something better out there and the only way to get it was to destroy and burn the path we were on. Yes, we are the romantics.

Plans B, C, D and E

This is my wish list. Don't laugh at it for it has been squeezed from my marrow and has the tenderness of those things that are fragile. I hope it will give someone the courage to write their own, no matter how silly the demands sound. I don't know how many of them will happen but here they are, listed out, in case the universe needs to double-check. At the end of life, when I demand why certain things weren't delivered to my doorstep, the powers that be can't say they forgot. For, in black and white, this has been printed and is waiting to come true.

Live in a house with a garden. Seeing the changes in nature helps me make peace with the changes in me.

Have kids. If I can't have my own, I will adopt. Simply because I think centring my life on just me will drive me cuckoo.

When the bills and mortgages are paid, I want to find meaningful work, which makes me feel justified about the space I take up on earth.

A Beetle. Bright, happy and yellow. Or a jeep. A rugged monster that eats up roads and distances proclaiming me as the queen of the terrain.

To live within walking distance from the sea, so I can hear the waves and listen to the whisperings of seashells.

Fish fry every single day.

Friends who are there for me as I am there for them. Who fill my space with happiness, who cheer me up and remind me with their calls I am not alone in a seemingly alone universe.

A cat. A dog. Dogs and cats. Mix them up. Little non humans who teach me love and love me without being taught.

Work and not have a job. Be independent of companies and bosses. Find a self-sustaining model of employment, where I am doing what I love fuelled by passion and not greed.

Wooden bookshelves filled with words that have taken me to different places. They are my treasures on earth, my provident fund for my old age and perhaps the best shrink I will ever find.

A soulmate/sexmate – the two-in-one not imported from Dubai. If this isn't possible then I'd wish to be a single woman who enjoys her singlehood and has no need for a better or a worse half.

Food that makes me think of food. I have never cooked in my life but I hope to be able to afford the good cook. If not, I will roll up my sleeves and figure out how to put those delicious morsels of heaven that tell you everything is okay with the world, day after day, on the table.

My parents in my life. We are independent of each other, yet dependent on one another. I have lived too long on my terms to live with them. Perhaps, it is the same for them as well. Or perhaps in the distant future they will move in with me and I will do for them what they did for me all their life – give love and care in unlimited supply.

Find the house in which I want to die. A place, where no matter where I go, it calls out to me as home.

Travel as far as I can and as often as I can afford to. For me, amongst all the activities we do as human beings, this is the one that makes the most sense. It leaves me with an indescribable feeling of gratitude and I understand how stupid we are to worry when a single eight-hour bus ride can change our world.

Intersections with brilliance. The good fortune of coming across minds in science, arts and in anything else that speaks genius. This association of people who are fuelled by a single purpose, driven by the one need to find a lost integer, will make me understand even if it's for the briefest instance what a privilege it is to be a human being.

Excellent single malts throughout my time on earth and no cholesterol to make me stop indulging in a little tipple at the end of that perfect or imperfect day.

Retire to a life of learning. In my old age, reread the philosophers, the spiritual giants, the master and teachers from different parts of the world and from multiple religions. For I am sure, even then I wouldn't have understood life. This will be the final attempt to do so.

Euthanasia. The minute I have a terminal disease, the path to death is a celebration. And when I can't take it anymore, I shun the hospitals and say 'hello morphine' with the cheerful bravado of a depressed clown who has a performance.

How many of these things will turn out to be real is a question only a time machine can answer. It doesn't matter though. For irrespective of what happens, what dreams materialize and what shatter, I will be happy. My divorce is a guarantee of that. I have chosen to leave someone for I believed that my life wasn't worth being spent enveloped by the tentacles of compromise. I have to make sure every day is a valediction of this.

It isn't easy. There is a secret life of sorrow divorcees go through. That numbness I carry at my rejection is so fundamental that it will always be a part of me. The pain of those years will never be flushed away and forgotten, but it won't hurt as much. Of late, my cross has gotten lighter too. It is baggage I carry effortlessly. I can toss it in the air, catch it, swing it and then tuck it back, hardly cringing at its scarred surface.

I will always remember how the biggest relationship in my life had shattered but I won't remember it every day. Yes, on that occasional rainy day the tears may fall, but the next day they would have dried up and my smile would dance into the world – not forced but naturally.

Plan A is already forgotten, a bad dream I woke up from. There is much more happening in Plan B and if for some reason that disintegrates, there is always Plan C, D, E and F.

Write down your wish list in the space on the next page. Forget about the Ex, about revenge, about pain. The worst is already over. Now things can only get better. You just have another thirty or forty odd summers, winters, monsoons and springs. Doesn't that sound like an incredibly small number? Just forty more twelfth of Augusts in our life. Just forty more celebrations that will mark the passing of time. Just forty more dances in the first rains of the monsoon. What are you going to do in that time?

I Wish For:

XII

THE ONE SECTION TO READ IF YOU CAN'T READ THE BOOK

The Balance Sheet of My Divorce

And in the end, all that I have lost, I have gained. Gained more, gained differently, gained again.

Loss: The ability to believe in the 'till death do us apart' promise. Suddenly, anything that has the promise of forever, smells suspiciously fake.
Profit: Understanding that permanence isn't necessarily 'a good thing' and knowing that the only permanent thing I have is me.

Loss: Invitations to weddings, first birthdays and other extended family gatherings.
Profit: Being spared the mind-numbing boredom that accompanies these functions.

Loss: Being a 'role' model to anyone under twenty.
Profit: Turning from 'aunty' to 'cool' to the same age group.

Loss: Half the rent.
Profit: Running a house the way I want.
Yes, the writing desk will be kept in the middle of the room and not in the conventional corner.

Loss: Friends who suddenly disappeared from my life citing excuses like their pepper-crusher had to be repaired! (For a year?!)
Profit: Discovering that true friendship is a friend who leaves his puppy at your place to 'baby-sit' for he heard the loneliness in your voice that day.

Loss: Being hurt by people who judge you and losing your happiness to them.
Profit: The understanding that doing the thing that will get me their approval will kill me.

Loss: Confidence in my attraction.
Profit: Figuring that it doesn't matter.

Loss: Trusting my judgement in men. How will I know for sure that this is the right one?
Profit: Trusting my strength, for when push came to shove, I stood.

Loss: A piece of my heart that is hurt beyond repair.
Profit: A bruised piece of my heart, which is a warning and a guarantee that my heart will survive.

Loss: My parents' happiness, especially with reference to their peers.
Profit: The absolutely wonderful, gratifying and comforting knowledge that they will stand by me no matter what.

Loss: Time.
Profit: The effort not to screw up what is left of time.

Loss: My child-bearing years.
Profit: The desire to have a child.

Loss: Money. Divorces are expensive.
Profit: Freedom. Any amount of money can never compensate the lack of it.

Loss: A good marriage.
Profit: Finally, I know what a good marriage is.

Loss: A house 'We' built.
Profit: A house 'I' built.

Loss: Happiness.
Profit: The striving towards happiness, for I know its value.

Loss: The tag of a 'good girl'.
Profit: The loss of tags.

Loss: The ability to depend completely on anyone.
Profit: The ability to depend on myself.

Loss: Everything on the drawing board.
Profit: Draw the patterns I like on it.

Loss: Love. Faith. Trust. In Him.
Profit: Love. Faith. Trust. In Me.

Loss: Innocence.
Profit: Wisdom.

Loss: One husband.
Profit: Myself.

In the end, when I calculate the losses and gains, I know I am extremely fortunate that I am divorced. I am not living a life trapped in a social web, caught in a cage of unhappiness, mediocrity and resignation. The worst of my single days were always better than the worst of my married days. The unasked punch in my stomach had dislodged the bone from my throat. This second chance is not something many people get. Today, I live better and happier, working furiously to make something out of who I am. Today, I know as long as I have my sanity and my life, I can conquer the world. Today, I am not just a divorcee. I am a divorcee who dances.

The Divorcee's Twelve-step Tango

If you've managed to reach here, reading all the words along the way, you don't need to read this chapter. However, if you are one of those non-readers who bought the book thinking it would help but just couldn't go through the entire thing, then I will beg you, not on my knees but with the conviction of a 'been-there, done-that', to take a quick look at what is written here. The alcoholics have their twelve steps to recovery. These are a divorcee's twelve steps to start dancing again:

I. *Let Go*

I couldn't force the Ex to love me or want to be with me. He wasn't showing any signs about needing to be together or even attempting to try and make the relationship work. I had to say goodbye to him or it would be a goodbye to the woman I was. Once my mind was made up about that, I focused on other things. I tried very hard to forget about blame – mine and his. Instead, I reminded myself that if the relationship was OVER, no amount of 'who is responsible' would bring it back. I had to rebuild my life and I had all the tools at my disposal. All I needed to do was pick them up.

II. *Get a Job*

I don't know if you are working, but if you are not, get a job. Any job. If you are, don't let go of that job. If neither situation is possible – volunteer five days a week to whichever charity you like – dogs, kids, old people – there are so many beings worse off than us, trust me. It is critical for you to step out of the house every day. My job was a saviour I could count on. It helped me keep my dignity; I didn't have to ask anybody for money (including the Ex, excluding one friend, for a haircut, details in Section IX). The job also made sure that my head wasn't in the debilitating world of the failed marriage. I had deliverables that were outside the emotional circus. If I didn't complete them, my boss would kick my ass. Every day, Monday to Friday, thanks to the job, there were large amounts of time when I didn't even remember the Ex (We, who are going through/have gone through a divorce know what a luxury this is).

III. *Walk/Exercise*

Every day for an hour. If that is too much, cut it down to a half hour: walk, jog, dance (take Sundays off, even the Lord rested on this day, remember). Do some physical activity that will make you sweat. I used to walk home from work. It saved taxi money, helped me see more of the world and less of 'poor me' and all those steps healed me along the way.

IV. *Take Care of Yourself*

Dress-up, look good. I don't mean look good in the conventional sense but in your head you should feel that you are attractive. If you don't, fix it either with external tools like clothes, parlour visits, shoes and haircuts. Or with internal tools like talks to yourself, reading about healing, learning something new.

V. *Fake Happiness*

Stop crying, start smiling. You may not feel like it, but grin, pretend to grin. Go out with your siblings, your friends, people in your age group. This fake happiness has a surprising way of turning real. This is one of my favourite divorce lessons. I had stumbled on it by chance, while making faces in the mirror as I cried. I noticed that when I smiled the tears would flow but they would lose their hold over me.

VI. *Close Contact*

I had to stop speaking and interacting with the Ex for a large period of time to feel my normalcy. If you think this will help, do the same. The problem with talking to the Ex is that we have been conditioned to be dependent on him for an extraordinarily long period of time. The mind will want to keep going back to him as it is the easiest and the most familiar support system we have in the universe. We have to break that. Contrary to popular opinion, unknown devils are better than known ones.

VII. *You Are Lucky*

I had to constantly remind myself how lucky I was. It was easy. Around that time, a friend of mine was diagnosed bipolar. Another died from a heart attack at forty. I had my sanity and my brains and with that I could conquer the world. So don't let anyone stand in the way of your moving on, especially someone who has hurt you.

VIII. *Think of College*

Think of a time when you were happiest and what sort of person you were at that time and then try to recreate that YOU. It isn't 100 per cent possible, but if I can get even fifty per cent of that joie de vivre I will consider myself blessed. (If the happy times were with your partner, think about what you did during those times – travelled, spoke up, sang karaoke without a gun to your head – and recreate them.) I think we forget that experiences are also about places and the 'newness' of things and not just about people.

IX. *Go to a Counsellor*

If you feel that the burden of unhappiness is too much, don't feel shy about speaking to a psychiatrist, though be careful if you do. Husbands, psychiatrists and pills are very easy to get dependent on. And our minds are always stronger than we think.

X. *It's Okay to Hurt*

The pain will be there, like it is eating you from the inside. Let it hang in you, it doesn't matter. It will go away one day without warning. Just don't let it stop you. If you can, ignore it.

XI. *Things Will Get Better*

The reason for the divorce was the worst thing that could have happened. Nothing will be that bad ever again. Life has no choice but to go upwards, to improve as it has already hit the lowest of the lows.

XII. *Have Fun*

It's okay. You deserve to.

Acknowledgements

Thank you my extended, beautiful family – Susheelchechi, Shantichechi, Rekha, Radhi, Raghu, Radu, Ashwini, Arun, Lakshmi. Uncles, aunts and cousins, who were gentle when times were tough.

Thank you Pranav Kumar Singh for trusting an unknown writer's story and shepherding the edit with utmost sensitivity and kindness.

Thank you Sushmita Chatterjee and the entire team at Pan Macmillan India who worked on making my manuscript a printed book.

Thank you Shruti Debi for believing in the book and championing it right from the very beginning.

Thank you R Sukumar and Priya Ramani of Mint Lounge for publishing my weekly column *Dancing Divorcee*, which was the genesis of this book.

Thank you my friends, who taught me I can't be sad forever – Dran, Roopz, Deepu, Anushka, Tarun, Iswar, Gautam (Peter), Kanchana, Arth, Leela, Pritha, Zarine, Rajiv, Amba, Aniruddha (Karim), Srija, Ramu, Aruna, Renu, Indu, Zaheer, Arup, Bijoy, Rocky, Dipti, Bops, Nithin (Arun), Ogo, Parvez, Anish and Bin.